T̶ꞁꞁᴏᴡ

HOW JIMMY JOHN WON
HIS CLOAK OF FREEDOM

The Story of a Teenaged Freed Slave
and the Connecticut Civil War Soldier
Who Brought Him North

by Dorothy Phillips Mobilia

Enjoy!
Dorothy Mobilia

1

How Jimmy John Won His Cloak of Freedom

FIRST EDITION

Cover: Images from an 1865 photograph on file in the Wilton Historical Society's collection at the Wilton Library, of "Jimmy John" and Cpl. Charles F. Hallock, Co. E Fifth Regiment, Connecticut Veteran Volunteers, First Brigade, First Division, Twentieth Army Corps, General Sherman's Army.

Printed by CreateSpace, An Amazon.com Company

This book is dedicated
to the real
Deacon John D. Taylor
(Jimmy John) (circa 1848-1930)
and
Charles F. Hallock
(Cpl. Charley) (1844-1917)

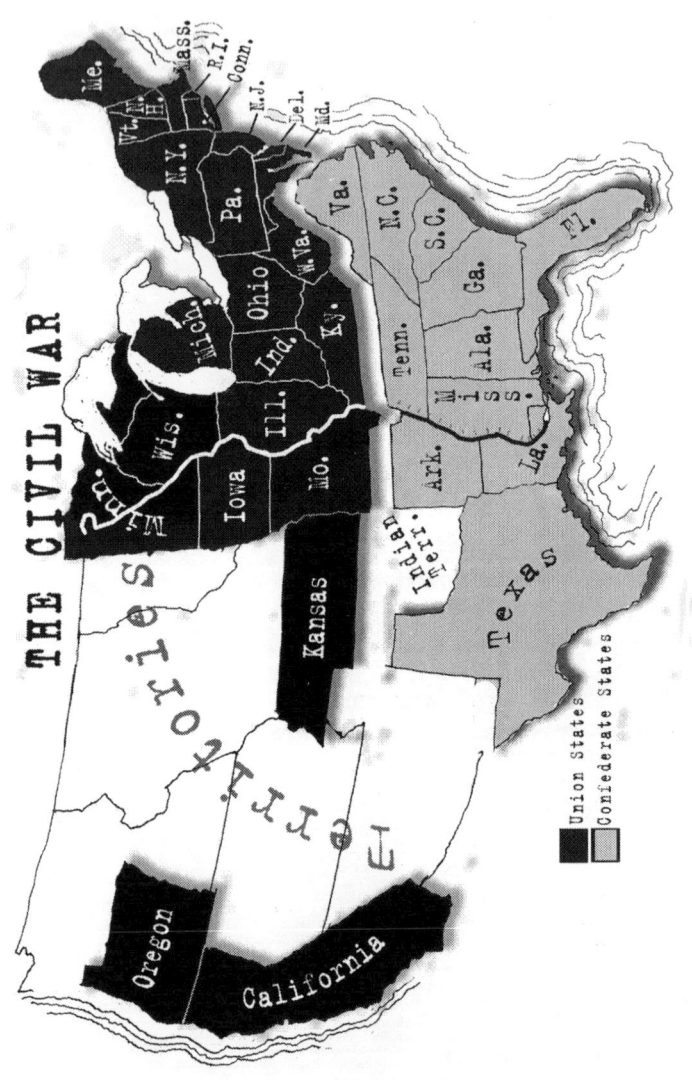

THE CIVIL WAR

Me. Mass. R.I. Conn. N.J. Del. Md. Vt. N.H. N.Y. Pa. W.Va. Va. N.C. S.C. Ga. Fl. Ohio Ky. Tenn. Ala. Mich. Ind. Miss. Ill. Ark. La. Wis. Iowa Mo. Minn. Kansas Indian Terr. Texas

Oregon California

Territories

Union States
Confederate States

1

South Norwalk, September 1917

Deacon Taylor raised his head and focused on the boy climbing the steps to the front porch. He shielded his eyes from the broad September sunshine and could make out Jesse, from next door.

"Deacon?" Jesse asked softly. "Don't mean to wake you. Just brought *The Hour* up from the sidewalk, so you wouldn't have to go down the steps with your cane and all."

"Jesse, thank you. The Lord bless you for small favors. You have a minute? To maybe read me the headlines and save me the trouble going inside and searching for my glasses?"

"I have time, Deacon." The boy giggled when the deacon stretched his arms and let out a noisy yawn. The deacon chuckled with him.

"I had me a nice little nap, rocking in the sun, and I feel the Lord's strength back in me. Come, sit in the other rocking chair and tell me the biggest story on the front page. I'm proud you can do something at age twelve that I couldn't do until I was sixteen."

Jesse scanned the page. "Well, suh, the biggest story, right at the top, is about Mr. Charles Hallock, from over on Flax Hill. He passed last night."

"Dear God, Jesse, read me the headline."

"Well, it's a big one. Got four lines to it."

Jesse looked questioningly at the Deacon, who nodded. He turned his eyes back to the page.

"Starts off, 'Mr. Hallock Goes to Great Beyond.'

"The second line reads, 'One of Norwalk's Grand Old Men Passes Away After Long Illness.'

"The next says, 'Civil War Veteran; Took Part in Public Affairs.'

"The last line says, 'Interested in All Local Matters and Voice Heard on Many Occasions.'"

The Deacon put a hand over his eyes. He heard Jesse's alarmed voice.

"You OK, Deacon?"

"Hm? Yes. He was a good friend. Brings back many powerful memories. He probably saved my life when I was just a little older than you."

Jesse was quiet for a minute. Then he said,

"Didn't he have something to do with the library? And politics here in town?"

"Yes to both, Jesse. He was the first president of the library and a city councilman for years. But our friendship goes back much longer than that, and to a place 500 miles away, in North Carolina, when I was, maybe fifteen or sixteen, and he was a Union soldier not much older than me."

"I know you was a slave once, but I never heard you talk about Mr. Hallock." Jesse frowned.

"No? Charley Hallock was a great hero to me in the biggest adventure of my life. He helped me put on my Cloak of Freedom."

He smiled at Jesse's wide-eyed look.

"I see I need to tell you more. Let me start with what Charley told me about how he got to North Carolina in the first place."

2
South Norwalk September 1861

The air was clear and warm this mid-April morning. Charley Hallock jogged easily along the half mile to work.

The husky sixteen-year-old had left home early. He hurried to meet up with friends for a little fun before the factory whistle signaled the beginning of another long day polishing locks at The Norwalk Lock Company.

He worked there for nearly four years now.

The job was way better than wading through the bone-chilling waters along the Connecticut shore of Long Island Sound, scooping up oysters for one long summer after leaving school when he was twelve. It also beat hauling merchandise on his father's packet boat.

He heard about the factory job through his friend, Ned, one of the first hired by The Lock Company when it opened that same year on the South Norwalk waterfront. It was a grand factory, the biggest by far in town, with hundreds of workers. Ned alerted Charley that there was an opening on the bench.

"The pay is OK and you get raises according to how well you do," Ned said.

Charley jumped at the chance. He argued with his disappointed father that he was probably the worst hand on the boat crew and could do less harm somewhere else. Besides, working in a factory was the modern way to get ahead. His father reluctantly gave in.

"You have to settle down soon, son," William Hallock warned. "Just be sure you apply yourself better than you have on the boat. You'll have only so many chances to prove yourself useful."

Charley was glad he wouldn't be under his father's strict eye at the factory.

Ned met him at The Lock Company door that first morning.

They walked past the two massive steam engines that powered the various lathes around the building. Foremen and workers strode quickly all around him, yelling to each other above the noise, opening doors that let out bursts of hammering and steam and strange industrial smells.

Charley was pushed back by the shock of the noise of metal grinding against metal, the odors of chemicals and molten metals, and the heat of the great iron furnace.

They reached the brass finishing room. Ned introduced him to his boss, Mr. Howe, who showed him the table stacked with newly cast brass locks, dull and rough.

"In the beginning, you'll learn how to file and sand pieces like these to get rid of the coating and rough edges. Then you move them on to the boys over there." He gestured to the second bench of workers. "They apply belts and wheels to buff and polish them." He showed Charley a finished lock, gleaming and sleek.

Mr. Howe guided Charley through the process. "It's important that you keep up with every one else," he said sternly. "There's no time to slack off. There are many steps, and each boy depends on the worker before him. No fooling around, either. You're not a school kid anymore."

Charley wondered, did he talk like that to all new boys, or had his father had a word with him?

He looked nervously toward the filers on the bench, then relaxed. He knew them all. Most were from the neighborhood or had gone to the same

Union School at one time or another. There was no time to talk, with the foreman standing right there, but they gave Charley a quick grin before bending over their work again.

He learned right away that first morning that Mr. Howe wasn't kidding. The pace was intense.

To make one and a half cents, Charley had to produce a dozen locks sanded to Mr. Howe's satisfaction. He was hard to please.

"Our locks are in demand overseas, in markets in England and France," the foreman said. "And they accept only perfect work."

Those early days, Charley didn't have time to think about new aches in his back and arms, how his eyes sometimes burned and teared, or how his hands got cut and coarsened. He was just worried he would be fired. The foreman already warned him the first week that he was making too many mistakes.

But friends made up for the long hours and the dusty, acrid-smelling room. As soon as the foreman stepped away, they shouted jokes and insults back and forth, barely above the noise of the belts and pulleys. They competed to see who could finish more pieces in a day. They dreamed up pranks at the bench and on the way home.

Gradually he caught on and did as well as most, and better than some. He took pride as his skills improved. He liked working with his hands, taking something rough and shaping it into something beautiful and useful. He also was proud of his calloused hands, a badge of a workingman.

Now, five months before turning seventeen, the once-scared kid had grown to a manly five-feet-eight inches and his upper lip showed a light fuzz that promised to grow into a sandy mustache, like his father's. Charley liked to dress well, and he was saving for a new silver watch.

These days, he sometimes shook his head when he looked down the bench at the new twelve-year-olds. Did he really ever mess up like that?

This April morning, he sensed something was different on the way to the factory. He could hear excited voices and cheers as he approached the red brick buildings lining the shore.

He turned onto Washington Street. Above the boat whistles and the click of horses' hooves on the cobblestones, he could swear he heard a fife and drum.

He headed for Marshall Street, hurrying now. A crowd swelled near the the old pottery factory by the railroad tracks.

He was startled to see The Bank of Norwalk president, Ebenezer Hill, standing in his open carriage in the center of the crowd, gesturing and talking loudly. His son, Eben Jr. steadied the horse.

Young Eben called out to Charley in excitement.

"You hear the news? Those rebels in South Carolina captured Fort Sumter on Saturday. We're at war! President Lincoln wants the northern states to raise 75,000 men to volunteer for three months to go down South to put down the rebellion. The governor's already put out a recruitment call to all the towns."

Charley tried to understand.

"Fort Sumter is a federal fort," Eben answered impatiently. "Attack the government, you declare war."

There had been talk around town for years that the states couldn't agree on which ones could have slavery and which ones couldn't. *The Gazette*, South Norwalk's weekly newspaper, buzzed about each new argument. Still, most Norwalkers brushed off the arguments. "Just politics," they complained.

The talk didn't mean much to Charley. There was no slavery in Connecticut. Hadn't been for years.

But now there was an actual rebellion, an attack on federal land, in the Southern states?

The men milling outside the pottery factory expressed shock and anger that the South actually wanted to split the country over a disagreement.

Charley pressed closer to hear Eben's father introduce Rev. T. I. Wooley, his own pastor at the First Methodist Episcopal Church. The pastor declared that the Fort Sumter attack was an attack on God and country. He waved his arms and punched the air, urging the crowd to rally with President Lincoln. Charley listened with rising excitement.

Heated discussions broke out. Some listeners argued that they and their sons shouldn't mess in this business. Others said the call was only for three months. They could bring sense to the South through the might of the Union and be back before the summer was over.

More and more, the talk shifted to the idea that war was a necessary evil to keep the country whole. They were fired up by the thought that the survival of the Union depended on bringing the rebel states in line.

Through it all, the Hills, father and son, rounded up volunteers. Spellbound, Charley watched oystermen, hatters, carpenters, neighbors all, shouting and cheering and marching toward the train station to enlist.

Mr. Hill led the parade to board the train. They were on their way to the state capitol, Hartford.

The train pulled out, the volunteers hanging out of the windows, waving and singing the Battle Hymn of the Republic along with the bystanders cheering and singing on the platform.

Charley had never seen anything like it. The city sometimes seemed almost too slow to make a decision about city matters. And now men were so fired up that they left without even talking it over with their families.

Older men leaned on their canes and looked on with longing. Charley heard them talking among themselves.

"We can help in other ways, especially with our money," one shopkeeper said. "We need a plan to help pay these young heroes and their families."

Charley heard later that Mr. Hill gave ten dollars to every Norwalk volunteer. It was the only money they would get until they received their first military paycheck. For privates, as most of them would be, that was thirteen dollars for the month.

Even the Fairfield County Bank offered a $30,000 loan to the governor to help equip the troops.

Charley's head and heart pounded. A chance to serve his country! Three months, settle everything back the way it was, and be back home. Meanwhile, have a little excitement, travel to places he had never been and might never get to otherwise.

If only he were twenty-one.

At work, the chatter continued the whole day, even with Mr. Howe standing next to the bench, listening.

That night, at supper, Charley brought up the President's call for volunteers.

Dad, without missing a beat as he cut up stew meat, shook his head.

"Those young men are going off on a lark, nothing more. This will never be a war. That's like relatives fighting relatives. Maybe there'll be a face-off, but that's all.

"But Dad, how can you say that? Everybody in town is up in arms. The Hills wouldn't let their workers go off on a lark, much less pay them for leaving. It's for keeping the country whole."

"Son, I can't answer why the Hills are supporting this foolishness. There will be no war, and all these men running off to a fight, sounds to me like they just want a little excitement. I can't take them seriously."

3
The Plantation

South Norwalk, 1917

I stretched on the rocker to get the ache out of my bones.

"My throat is getting dry. Jesse. Could you bring us that pitcher of lemonade from the icebox? And glasses? It's a warm day for September and you're probably as thirsty as I am."

Jesse returned quickly with the lemonade.

"Deacon Taylor? What did Mr. Hallock do then?" he asked between gulps.

"I'll get to that. But in our conversations, Charley Hallock asked me many times to tell him what was going on at the plantation about that time. He wanted to understand how slaves lived.

"I explained that the plantation owner, Mr. McPherson, was not one of them kindly masters. Marse kept us in line. The Missus of the house was a little softer, at least before things got really bad."

I recalled a time when I was eleven or twelve. I was never sure exactly how old. But it was right after the fort was captured in South Carolina.

I was "Jimmy John" then, resting under the shelter of a big old ash tree to stay out of the blistering sunlight. I must have dozed off.

A searing pain across my legs jolted me awake.

I rolled away from the tree and tried to catch my breath. The whip came down again, across my back.

"I don't give you food and a roof to sleep under, to have you snore away under a tree in the middle of the day," swore Marse. "You cost me more than you're worth. Now get back in that field and chase those damn crows. You and your kind are gonna cost me this crop if you keep this up."

I heard the whip whistling toward me again and struggled against the pain to get up. I slipped out of the way just as the nine tails snapped at the grass just behind me.

"Sorry, Marse. Sorry. Sorry," I gasped.

I ran, limping, out into the field, where the boys waved hands and sticks at the birds bothering the tall corn stalks, trying to peck the ripening ears open. They was smart, those crows. They knew the corn was getting ready for eating.

Lots of times, they'd peck the seeds right out of a newly planted furrow, or even peck at the green ears. At harvest, the field was black with them.

Seemed to me that fighting crows would be my job for life. I couldn't remember a time when I wasn't chasing them fearless birds. Or being chased by Marse. I was an easy target, small as I was.

Not everyone picked on me. The Missus liked to work in the house garden, and sometimes called on me to help. She had me picking stones and sometimes taught me numbers and even showed me how to read and write some. Slaves wasn't supposed to know how to do those things.

Sometimes she talked almost like I was one of her children. Almost.

I even asked her, with a little laugh, "Missus, is you my momma?"

"What nonsense." She leaned against her rake. "Don't be disrespectful. Besides you know very well who your momma is."

I did know, barely. My family was a gang of four brothers and six sisters. I was the runt, the one who had to run out of everyone's way. The one the brothers smothered in the bed. When they started their kicking, I'd roll to the floor, and sleep there, using my pants and shirt as a pillow. But my mama? She was long gone, sold to another family, somewhere.

Now they was all gone to other plantations.

I asked Missus, anyway, "Well, tell me again who I is."

She leaned over the rake and ruffled my hair.

"Your daddy's Daniel McPherson. We sold him to a South Carolina plantation owner along with five other slaves. Your momma, of course, is Millet Grain. We got her when she was a teenager. She and Daniel grew your whole family with us.

"Eventually your momma was sold to a Georgia master. You was a baby, and the owner didn't want to take you. One or another of the women filled in until you was old enough to take care of yourself."

I remembered. It was a sadness and a loneliness deep inside that just about every slave friend woke up to every day. It was pain that only prayer and singing to God around the fire at night after supper could ease. We was all in this together, and somehow the singing and praying together made it bearable.

"Anyway, that was a long time ago," Missus said. Her words brought me back. I began nipping again at the weeds just coming up.

"I reckon you'll be with us a while longer," she said. "You'll be ready to take on manly jobs here soon, or be sold to another master. You're a hard worker when you put your mind to it."

She stood up. "We're done here. Now scoot off to the fields. During the week, I expect you to keep an eye out for any new weeds that take a fancy to planting themselves here."

I headed to the fields, spotting where Marse was waving that whip at someone else. He was in a mean mood this morning. I detoured to my favorite ash tree and climbed high this time, settling on a wide branch. I needed to think over my situation.

I made sure to act smiley and happy around Missus, but now a cloud and a burning settled over my head and heart. Seemed like I didn't belong to anyone as kin. My family was the other boys my age who wrassled with me and chased crows. I barely remembered my real brothers and sisters.

Shadowy memories of my broad-shouldered Papa and my sweet Mama, and the terror when each of them was lost to me, flooded my mind.

I day-dreamed of being my own person instead of having to obey someone else all the time, somebody who waved a whip at me to make sure I remembered who was boss.

Then I thought about the day Papa took me aside, just before he went to auction.

"I ain't got much time here," he said desperately. "Don't know where I'll be after tomorrow. But I need to pass on something that you tell no one but your own children one day, as long as you is a slave. Understand?"

I stared at Papa, whose eyes turned steely.

"Understand?" he repeated.

I nodded. I was scared by the way he was talking.

"No way is your name or mine McPherson. Our people brought over here had no last names. But in the white man's way, we was given the names of our masters, our owners.

"Your granddaddy had the name of his master. But he told me one day, like I'm telling you, that if he had to have a last name, he would pick the name of somebody he respected. That name is Taylor, and I'm telling you that's my real last name too, and it's yours."

I scrunched my face and stared into his eyes. "Who is this Taylor?"

"He never said. But you talk with the other slaves sometime and they will own up to having a private name. Inside, they are someone that can't be sold.

"Taylor is your name, son, your one free thing while they try to own you, your thoughts, and your body. For two generations it's been taken by your blood family and secretly handed down. Just keep it to yourself, or you lose this one little bit of freedom, something they don't know about you."

The next day, like we feared, Papa was sold away.

"Taylor" became my salvation in the worst of times, especially after the whippings. I clung to that little bit of freedom Papa handed me.

Lately, some slaves thought their lives might change. I couldn't help but hear Marse and the other plantation owners cussin' about the North interfering in the way they did business. Slavery was necessary, they said, and the southern states had the right to own slaves so's they could run the plantations. But the states in the north, who didn't know squat about plantation life, said people could not own people. Heck, the owners answered back, slaves ain't people.

"And those northerners are hypocrites," Marse said. "Their big clothing mills like the cotton from the southern plantations well enough."

Talk really picked up when Abraham Lincoln was sworn in as President of the United States this year. Marse didn't like him at all. Mr. Lincoln kept pushing about getting rid of slavery.

The slave states said otherwise. They had rights. It was all there in the Constitution. It was now in their own Constitution of the Confederate States of America.

Us slaves got excited and fearful when the CSA got formed and attacked Fort Sumter. Something had to bust.

Sure enough, the President wouldn't let that stand. And when he called for a volunteer army to bring the Southern states in line, that's when North Carolina went over to the Confederacy, too.

Right away, the Union army took over the border states and blockaded the ports. The President wanted that the Confederate states couldn't sell their products anywhere, and would have to come back under the Union.

For slaves like me, all this politicking made life a little bit worse.

Whenever Marse heard us whispering, he pulled out his whip.

"Don't you even think about running to the North," he would yell. "Right is on our side, and you can't go anywhere. You belong here, you will be brought back here, or be shot for trying to leave."

I knew that wasn't just a threat. I knew slaves who had run. They was always brought back and punished real bad as an example to other slaves thinking of running, maybe even to Canada. No slavery there.

I would play it safe and stay put.

All that thinking made me sleepy. I dozed in the soft breeze and the rustling leaves around me, but my eyes flew wide open at the sound of Marse calling out my name in that blood curdling voice of his. As soon as he went storming in the opposite direction, I slipped out of the tree, grabbed an old stick and headed toward a knot of boys running in the south field. Soon I was yelling with them, chasing those crafty birds.

Now, today, on my porch in South Norwalk, I rested my glass on my knee and turned to Jesse. "No sir, that was no time for me to get fancy ideas. Meanwhile, that year, 1861, Charley Hallock had his own decision to make."

4
Charley Enlists

Some days Charley thought of little else but the Union army. It was already July, and friends and neighbors who signed up for ninety days were expected home soon. The war was on but not much was happening for the Connecticut volunteers.

The Gazette, the local weekly, came every Tuesday with news from Washington and the front. The editor, Aaron Homer Byington, also was a Washington correspondent for *The New York Tribune* and a Union supporter. He even joined the military unit guarding the nation's capitol until the volunteer troops arrived.

Charley read Byington's dispatches eagerly for the facts as the community speculation and gossip grew intense.

Letters arrived daily in town from men who had enlisted and were still in camps in the state and anxious to get to the front. At work, Jeb Smith read letters from his brother, Sam, to bench mates during lunch break.

Even Mr. Howe listened.

Sam said they learned quickly that the army was not ready for them. The men who dropped everything and took the train to the state capital to enlist found there were no guns and no uniforms. Some men hung around the campgrounds, drilling, or came home for a day or two at a time.

"Mostly we drill, march, and play baseball. We talk with soldiers from other towns in Connecticut around the fire at night and play cards," Sam wrote. "The musicians play marches and we sing along. Hope there'll be real action soon. We only have days before we get mustered out."

Some volunteers made it to Washington, D.C.

They met soldiers from all around the Union. Starting as strangers, they became brothers, training together to face a common enemy.

One day after work, Eben Hill Jr. pulled his carriage to the side of the road and called out to Charley. The war was on both their minds.

"I wish I were old enough to go," Charley confessed. "It could be the chance of a lifetime."

Eben agreed. "It's worse for me," he said. "I'm a year younger than you. Who knows if I'll ever go?"

Then the unbelievable happened.

The dispatch said that in the first real battle of the war, the Rebels humiliated Union forces near a railway station at Manassas, in Virginia. The Union army called the place Bull Run, for the name of the river running through the field.

One of The Lock Company filers brought *The Tribune* to the shop. Charley crowded with the others to read the details.

Hundreds of men, women and children had gathered at the battlefield to watch the action.

Like it was a show.

Union Gen. Irvin McDowell led 34,000 green troops against the Virginia soldiers who marched there under command of Gen. Pierre G. T. Beauregard or who rode there by railroad under the command of Gen. Joseph Johnston. The report said the Rebels came charging down a slope, yelling a blood-curdling roar that stunned the Union forces before they could recover and strike back.

Repulsing repeated Union charges, one Rebel brigade stood firm under the command of Gen.

Thomas J. Jackson who, *The Tribune* noted, quickly got the nickname, "Stonewall." Even by the time Gen. Johnston's troops came on the battlefield, the North was losing.

Another Confederate general, J. E. B. Stuart, and his cavalry captured the Union artillery.

Some 3,000 Union men were killed or wounded before the remaining federal troops turned and ran back across the river, dropping equipment and supplies as they retreated along the road to Washington D. C.

"No!" Charley cried out as he read. One of the Union men captured and dragged off to Libby Prison, an old warehouse in Richmond, Virginia, was David O'Connor of the Third Norwalk Volunteers.

Bull Run was a rousing victory for the Rebels, even though they lost 2,000 men.

Byington wrote that the onlookers and officials in Washington D.C. were shocked by the bloody outcome.

The newspaper was passed from hand to hand at The Lock Company. Workers read the words in silence.

"They died or ran away," one said, unbelieving.

The article said the President put out another call, this time for 300,000 volunteers, to serve for three years. He relaxed the minimum age to 18.

It hit Charley that Mr. Lincoln wasn't predicting this time how long the war would last. Certainly not just three months. His mouth went dry. Could the North really lose?

At home, Charley talked to his mother while she was making dinner.

"Ma, it's not going well."

"Well, thank goodness you're too young to go," she said.

"Dad could give me permission."

Charley, don't get any ideas. You stay here. You're the oldest and we need you."

"Ma, friends are at risk. We're in trouble, and the President is asking for our help."

"You'll lose your job if you go," she said. "How will we survive?" Then, "How will I survive if you get yourself killed?"

Charley put his arm around her shoulders. He looked down at her tearful, distressed face.

"There's Dad. There are people in town who have pledged to take care of families. My brothers will be old enough to work soon. And besides, you wouldn't have my mouth to feed."

She poked him gently and pressed her face into his shirt. He hugged her.

"Ma, this is the honorable thing to do. Even Pastor Wooley said we have to fight when words fail to win the argument. We can't let this country break up."

"Your father will talk more with you about this," she said softly, and turned back to the stove.

Charley went to his room. His roommate brother, Henry, fourteen, had not yet come home from his ballgame. Charley sat on the bed to think.

He was torn by not wanting to hurt his mother or cross his father. But they didn't hear the pastor's speech, or the shopkeepers and business-men or the men who rushed to volunteer.

The longer he thought, the surer he got. His parents would have to understand one day.

He ran down the stairs and headed for the door. "Be back by supper," he said before his mother could ask where he was going.

He raced to the train station and caught up with the enlistees milling around who signed up for three years with the Fifth Connecticut Volunteer Regiment. He spotted Charley Beers, also sixteen, who had his father's permission to go.

"Beers, you think they need more men to fill the regiment's quota?" Charley asked, desperately.

Beers nodded. "Probably. See that corporal over there? His name's Edward Nelson. I'll introduce you."

Straightaway, Nelson told Charley to meet him at ten o'clock that night to take the train to Hartford.

"Be sure you bring a letter from your father, saying it's OK for you to go," Nelson said as he turned to talk with the next person in line.

Charley's heart pounded. Tonight.

He didn't have much time.

He ran to the grocery store at Marshall and Main Streets and searched out the hat clerk, Jim Brown. Brown had a flair for for words, and fine handwriting. He was his father's age, but he was a friend.

"Jim, help me out. My father needs to sign a letter that gives me permission to enlist. You know his handwriting is not so good. Do me a favor and draw up something official looking. I need it right away so he can sign it before the recruits leave tonight."

"Lucky you," Jim said. "Wish I were young enough to go."

That night, Henry, happy and tired from the game and a big meal, fell asleep quickly. When the house grew quiet. Charley chucked his pajamas and dressed in the clothes he had piled by the foot of the bed. He patted his pants pocket. The unsigned paper was carefully folded inside.

He was relieved that Brown hadn't seemed suspicious.

Hardly daring to breathe, he slipped out and ran to the station.

Maybe fifty men and boys were there, talking excitedly about imagined feats of bravery to keep every star intact on the flag. Charley wondered how many fathers had signed for those who were underaged. But he didn't ask, and they didn't ask him, as they piled into the train.

They reached Hartford at two in the morning and were directed to a field of white tents in a lot at Bond and Webster streets. Charley was assigned to the huge, eighteen-man tent of Orderly Sgt. Munson Hoyt, also of Norwalk, the first sergeant among all the sergeants. Luckily, he didn't know the Hallock family that well and didn't recognize him.

The next morning Charley was sworn in by Col. Orris S. Ferry, a U.S. senator who joined as soon as the President called for volunteers. Charley was assigned to the regiment's Company E. Col. Ferry would be the regiment's commanding officer. A whisper of approval went around the group that this favorite son of South Norwalk would lead them.

Charley had forged his father's signature on his permission slip, but he decided at the last minute to tell officials he was nineteen. He received his uniform—light blue woolen pants, dark blue woolen coat and vest, grey felt cloth overcoat. So far, so good. The army was getting more organized since the time Sam had signed up.

Charley found everything about army order exciting.

Company E had about a hundred men and the Fifth Regiment had ten companies. The sergeant told them that the regiment would be part of a brigade, and three or four brigades would be assigned to a division. Three or four divisions made up a corps, and an army might have five or more corps.

Every soldier above private wore insignia according to his rank. Charley stayed alert to salute anyone with a chevron on his sleeve, or bars, oak leaves, eagles, on up to silver stars on their shoulders.

On the field, the sergeants drilled them for hours a day, grinding out marches while carrying rifles, bayonets, and fifty pounds of gear. Singing patriotic songs cheered them and helped them keep in step. Charley and the other raw recruits struggled to catch up with the men drilling since May.

Not that the sergeant missed a chance to tell them that they would never make the grade, that they were soft and undisciplined.

Still, he could feel a new hardness in the muscles in his arms and legs, and in his gut. He made mistakes, sometimes the same ones over and over. His only thought was that every day brought him closer to the fight.

A week later, they marched in single file past Col. Francis Loomis, a wealthy New London businessman and former state legislator who was elected to his military post. The word was that the colonel would question them about their age. Charley's heart was in his mouth. But the colonel just glanced at him in the line and told him to pass on.

So there he was, in uniform and sworn in, actually sixteen, but three years older on his enlistment papers.

The men and boys talked endlessly of plans to show the enemy that the Union would quickly end this ridiculous rebellion. Everyone would forget the disaster at Bull Run.

Finally they got the word they were waiting for: They were heading to the front.

"Our trip will be longer than usual, since the route going direct through Washington D.C. is taxed to the limit with troops," Sgt. Hoyt told them at muster July 27. "We'll take a roundabout way, but we'll get into action soon enough."

Two days later they tumbled out of the tents, quickly packed their gear and marched to the train depot. No time for breakfast.

Charley thrilled to the sendoff.

Music and cheering crowds led the way. The regiment got a heroes' farewell by the Putnam Phalanx, a military and social group that had honored soldiers since the American Revolution. In New Haven, a twenty-four-member band, on instruments paid for by Gov. William Buckingham himself, played patriotic marches to escort them from the station to the waterfront. Well-wishers lined the streets to the dock where the steamer, *Elm City*, waited to take them to Elizabethport, New Jersey.

Charley wished his father could see him now, and see how proud everyone was of the volunteers. No one thought they were off on a lark.

They were famished by the time they reached the Harrisburg depot and the local ladies served them coffee and lunch.

The next train crossed the Susquehanna River to Baltimore, Maryland.

They received their ammunition and loaded their rifles at the station.

"This city is loyal to the Union but there are plenty of Secessionist sympathizers here," the captain warned. "Keep your eyes open as we march across town to the Baltimore and Ohio Railroad depot, where we pick up our train for the final leg of this trip."

Charley warily watched the heavy crowds in the sweltering heat, but there were no signs of trouble this day.

The train waiting for them was a mix of passenger, box and freight cars. They were assigned to freight cars fitted out with boards as benches, and they settled in for the overnight ride to Sandy Hook, on the Potomac River, at the opposite side of the state. They were tired now, only occasionally making small talk and joking and complaining around turns that slid them to the other side of the benches.

Hours later, hot, bleary and aching, they emerged from the cars into a stunning setting.

"The Blue Ridge Mountains. They really look blue," Charley said in awe, looking up. Range after range, some with clouds nestled between, stretched as far as he could see.

The boys soon were on the march.

They halted at Pleasant Valley, and settled in at Camp Wooster at Sandy Hook with the Nineteenth New York Volunteers and regiments commanded by Maj. Gen. Nathaniel P. Banks, leader of the Army of Virginia. Charley's unit was part of the First Brigade, Second Corps.

The recruits set up rows of white tents around a drill field. Exhausted and hungry, Charley sat back at last to take in the scenery. It was late afternoon. The sky was filled with billowing white clouds. The Potomac was just in front of them. The Blue Ridge Mountains gazed down on them to the rear.

And the enemy was just across the river.

5
Typhoid

The camp was a buzzing hive the next morning. Drumbeats signaled when it was time for roll call, sick call, gathering firewood, hauling water, when it was time to eat.

Morning and afternoon, sergeants shouted as the boys in each company struggled to march as a unit. The sergeants swore that these volunteers, organized less than a month ago, would never be military. What could you expect from volunteers? Their language grew stronger, louder, as the recruits kept making the same mistakes they had back in Hartford.

In the background Charley could hear cavalry officers cussing at their recruits with the same exasperation when they didn't follow the buglers' signals.

After a full day of marching, Charley sat in front of his tent and gingerly pulled off his stiff low boots and poured cold water over his blistered feet. He had marched sixteen sweltering miles, loaded down with a backpack, haversack, blanket roll, rifle and bayonet. He sweated in his woolen uniform. His woolen cap was itchy.

His body remembered every mile. He had known pains from his long hours sitting at the bench at the factory, but this was different.

He looked around. The older men from his company, some already husbands and fathers, had gathered by their own fires. He wasn't ready to join them. There could be questions about his age, for one thing.

Recruits his age from his hometown straggled over—Oliver Brady, Nate Wheeler, Owen Murphy, Elijah Jones—and started a campfire.

Charley thought the sergeant was kidding when he said soldiers had to know how to cook their own food.

"Check your haversack," the sergeant barked. "You have a cookbook. There'll be a lot of times when you'll have to do your own meals. This is one of them."

He tried to follow directions. Funny how things didn't come out the way they sounded in the book.

But Oliver, Nate, Owen and Elijah were good company. They got the fire working and put the coffee pot on to boil. Like them, Charley hung his ration of salted meat on a stick he held over the flame. His mouth watered as the meat sizzled. But the beef turned out charred on the outside and raw inside. He ate it anyway. He ate carrots, uncooked, from the can. He ate his rock-hard square cracker called hardtack. He gulped down two tin cups of hot, sweet coffee to kill all the tastes.

"We've gotta do better than this," Elijah groaned.

"Yeah, we'll kill ourselves before the enemy has a chance to try themselves."

They heard a laugh and looked up.

"A home-cooked meal would be right just about now, eh, boys?"

The man looking down at them had a large mustache and floppy brimmed hat. He wasn't in a uniform.

The visitor extended his hand. "Henry C. Davis, at your service," he said smiling. "I'm the regiment's sutler, contracted to offer candy, butter, cheese and other delicacies that you won't find in your provisions. And the magazines and newspapers of the day."

The boys introduced themselves. Charley wondered what to say next. He had no money, yet. The sutler didn't seem to notice. He had plenty to say himself.

"Where're you from?"

"South Norwalk," Charley said.

"I've met a few of your friends already, at the other campsites," he said, waving his hand down the line of fires lighting the dusk. "I'm from just north of Norwalk proper. I run a grocery in the Winnipauk section, but my family has property the next town up, in Wilton. I signed up to bring supplies to the troops. I thought there'd be a need for extras here, while you brave young men fight to keep the country united."

Charley thought he detected a touch of sarcasm in the sutler's voice.

"Come by when you're ready," Davis said, moving on. "My tent is over by the supply wagons. Big sign out front. Can't miss it."

Charley was achingly tired. The others were already stowing the food they didn't eat and dousing the fire. They said their goodnights and moved into the tents.

In his, some men were already wrapped in their blankets, with only the rubberized sheet between them and the dirt. Charley stepped to the first row on the left and laid down his blanket. He heard his name called.

"Good to see you in this tent," Oliver murmured.

Charley turned to answer and heard a soft snore. He smiled and closed his eyes. Just like at home, sleeping with his brother. As long as he keeps it low like that, we'll get along.

He shook off the images of his family and the factory. He could deal with that later. He knew he was right to just leave and do his duty. Why didn't his father understand?

Over the next few days, there were always a few men who reported to sick call after assembly. The numbers kept growing. Dysentery. They got to calling it Soldier's Disease. No one knew what caused it—maybe it was the water or the food or the long hours with little rest.

Charley was not prepared to see some of them die.

Especially not Nate, the first casualty he knew personally. Nate was taken to the hospital in Baltimore and died within six weeks. He never had a chance to fire a single shot.

Not long after, the corps marched to Camp Ellsworth at Darnstown, Maryland, near the rest of

Gen. Banks troops. Charley awoke one morning, achy and vaguely not himself.

He reported for roll calls and drills as usual, but after a couple of days, the regiment's Capt. Wilson Wyant took one look at him, sweating and unsteady, and pronounced, "Typhoid Fever."

"Do we send you to the hospital or home, soldier?"

Nate had gone to the hospital and never left.

Charley thought dully about a showdown with his father if he went home. He was losing focus, felt hot and nauseous and suddenly intensely homesick.

"Home," Charley whispered hoarsely. The captain granted him furlough to recover.

He caught a ride on an army wagon going to Frederick, Maryland, some twenty-two miles east, to catch a train to Baltimore. A traveler approached him on the platform to thank him for serving.

"Aren't you going the wrong way,?" the man said smiling. "The war's the other way."

"I'm going home to Connecticut for awhile," Charley said. "Baltimore's my first stop."

The man shook his head. "The last train to Baltimore's already left. You'll have to wait until Monday."

Charley sagged against the bench.

The man came closer. "Say, you don't look well at all.

"Tell you what. Come home with me. You can stay over with my wife and me until Monday morning. It's the least we can do for a soldier in this war."

Charley tried to refuse but found himself led to a wagon and helped up on the bench seat. At the house, and over his halfhearted protests, they showed him to the guest room.

He sank into the bed and fell into a deep sleep almost immediately. He tossed feverishly during the night, aware vaguely that they were laying wet cloths on his burning forehead.

Monday, they took him to the station, and at Baltimore he managed to meet the train to Philadelphia. Passengers saw his uniform and offered him food, but just the smell made him ill.

At Philadelphia he caught a train to New York. Again, a passenger noticed his uniform and his sickness. And again, he missed his train. The last one for South Norwalk had already left.

"You can't stay here, soldier," the man said. "There's a small hotel nearby where you can wait overnight."

Charley didn't protest. He could barely stand.

At the hotel, the Good Samaritan paid for Charley's room and told the desk clerk to wake him in time for the morning seven o'clock train bound for Connecticut.

The knock on the door came awfully soon.

Charley had to rest on the curb just about every block on the way to the rail terminal, and he missed the early train. He made the one that came two hours later. Finally, he reached South Norwalk at eleven o'clock and a neighbor drove him home in his wagon.

Unsteady, he pushed through the kitchen door. The room was warm and filled with the aroma of food that somehow didn't seem to bother him.

His mother looked up from the stove, startled. "Charley? Oh my heaven, Charley. You've come home."

She ran to embrace him, then pulled back. "Why, you're burning up. What's wrong?"

He wasn't sure he answered, but when he awoke he was in his old bed and the sunlight outside was still bright. Dr. McClean, the family doctor, bent over him. His father sat in a chair on one side and his mother was on the other.

"Hello, son," his father said soberly. "Is this what the army did to you?"

Charley looked at him and closed his eyes. He started to speak, but his father interrupted.

"Don't say a word. We'll talk later. But it was a shock to find the note you forged, in the pocket of the pants you sent home from camp."

Charley shook his head. "Never used it. They believed me when I said I was nineteen." He closed his eyes.

When he awoke again he felt stronger, and got up and moved toward the murmuring voices in the kitchen.

"Charley!" called his sister Hattie. She ran over to hug him. His brothers, from Henry, fourteen, to Willie, eight, Moses, five, and baby George, shy at three, hung back at first. Then they had a dozen questions.

"Where were you?"

"Did you shoot anyone yet?"

"Can I try on your cap?"

"Are you home for good?"

He shook his head "no" at the last question and managed a grin. He sat down at the table, under the pressure of his mother's hand, and sipped from the cup of tea in front of him. The drink she always gave them when they were sick.

His father sat opposite, stone-faced.

Charley looked warily at his father. But there was a rising pleasure inside anyway. It was good to be home, even for a little while.

Hattie squeezed his hand.

"We're going to Capt. Russell's wedding tonight at the Congregational Church. Want to come?"

"John's getting married? I didn't know. He's an officer in the Eighth Infantry. I haven't seen him since, well, since I left."

He paused. "I'm feeling a little better. Maybe I can go."

His father frowned. "You're not in the best of shape."

Charley shrugged. "John's going into battle soon. I'd like to wish him well."

The wedding was joyful. Charley was in a glow from the neighbors' respect and curiosity about him and the other town boys serving with him. Returning home, bone-deep weariness took over.

He stayed in bed for weeks, shamelessly enjoying the rest and attention. His father asked him only how he felt, and never mentioned the war.

Charley grew stronger and his thoughts turned constantly to the regiment. He began to feel lazy that he was home while they were drilling, and maybe even fighting by now. September 9 rolled around and the family celebrated his seventeenth birthday.

He used the money gifts to buy himself a pair of comfortable shoes and, on impulse, the silver watch he always wanted. Still, his recovery time dragged.

Dr. McClean finally gave him a certificate of health in December.

Charley stopped by neighbors' homes to collect letters and keepsakes for sons and husbands in the regiment. His family was tearful when he left, but he already was impatient to see Oliver and the others, now at Camp Huntington in Frederick, Maryland.

Meanwhile, down in Bear Creek, I ran errands and such for the winter. The Missus acted distracted.

She said she didn't have time anymore for reading and writing. She didn't want to talk about it, and told me not to mention our lessons to Marse.

Marse didn't bother me much these days. He was in a right good mood. "That Stonewall," he would chuckle. "He's just too smart for them Yanks. Between Gen. Lee and him and Jeb Stuart, they don't have a chance."

I wondered whether the North had any surprises that would change Marse's mind.

I wondered how this war would affect me, one way or the other.

6
Stonewall Jackson

Just days after Charley rejoined, the regiment had orders to march toward the northern part of the state. The long, tiring hours were even tougher than he remembered. The weather was bitter cold now, and they tramped in the snow all day and sometimes at night in the rain.

The first night they stopped at a farm and set up camp on the frozen ground. Elijah had a better idea for Company E. "The top of that barn is filled with nice soft, warm hay," Elijah said. "Why should we crowd into a wet tent when we can sleep in the haymow?"

In the morning they congratulated themselves for the brilliant idea. But they had forgotten about their socks and shoes and boots, piled in wet mounds on the barn floor, and frozen as hard as stones.

The rest of the army was already packed and moving.

Panicked, the company ran painfully in bare feet to the farm house. The farmer shook his head at their pitiful state and let them thaw their shoes and dry their socks by the big iron kitchen stove. Sheepishly, they caught up with the others, jeering and laughing at them. Charley cheered up some by the time they reached Hagerstown, where housewives and girls greeted them with hot coffee.

They continued on to Williamsport, a town on the Potomac and a major port on the Chesapeake & Ohio Canal in Washington County, to serve guard duty along with the Thirteenth Massachusetts on the Maryland shore.

Their detail was ordered to watch out for Confederates at Dam No. 5, one of a series of dams diverting water from the river to the canal to bring coal to the Washington D.C. area and to provide a Union route for supplies and troops.

Maj. Gen. Thomas Jackson was the Rebel leader. His feats on the battlefield were glowingly described in the local newspapers they picked up along the way. Jackson had made fools of the Union troops at Bull Run when he was only a colonel and earned his nickname, "Stonewall." Now he was the commander of the Valley District, between the Blue Ridge and Allegheny Mountain ranges.

From their vantage point, the Union detail could make out enemy cavalry pickets patrolling the Virginia side.

Impulsively, Charley and his companions aimed their muskets across the water and shot.

It was a dumb move—the armies were nearly a mile apart and the weapon range was only seventy-five feet. Charley was disgusted that he wasted thirteen rounds.

Stonewall's men did destroy the dam but pulled back when Union reinforcements arrived and their guns drew within range. While Jackson's men claimed a brief victory, the Union troops quickly repaired the damage.

"Maybe this Stonewall isn't all he's rumored to be," Charley suggested.

Oliver shook his head. "He has a reputation of being tricky."

The Fifth Connecticut marched that winter for guard duty assignments all around northern Maryland. They often backtracked, from Hagerstown to Williamsport to Clear Spring, to Hancock to Frederick City, Hancock, again to Hagerstown, Clear Spring and Hancock.

Charley's shoes shrank painfully in the ankle-deep snow and he cut the leather to make them wearable until he was issued a pair of Army boots. The new boots weren't much better, and fell apart after two weeks.

March 11, the regiment set up camp for the night outside Winchester, Virginia, where Stonewall had his headquarters. The Confederate town was important because of a railroad, roads and turnpikes to both Washington D.C. and Richmond, the Rebel headquarters. It was the county seat and a market center.

This time the colonel announced they should be ready to take the town the next morning.

"Ready for our first battle?" Oliver asked at the campfire, boiling a pot of coffee.

Charley, cleaning his rifle, was confident. "We won't run away like some we've heard about." He volunteered to be one of the thirty men to skirmish ahead of the troops into Winchester. His heart pounded as they got closer and formed their line of battle.

But they never fired a shot.

No enemy. Stonewall had withdrawn his men out of the city and slipped back to the valley.

Disappointment gave away to relief and the Union army spent the next two weeks in and around Winchester. One volunteer in Company F was a printer by trade and started up a weekly paper, *The Fifth Connecticut.*

He observed that they were meeting up with slaves in Virginia.

"Some of the Secesh hereabouts told their slaves that the Yankees were of a different race from the Southerners and had horns on their heads," he wrote. "The darkies believed it (and their masters have been in the habit of swallowing bigger lies in *The Winchester Virginian*) and are astonished not to see these appendages."

In mid-April Charley wrote home:

"Stonewall returned to Winchester last month with 7,000 men when most of our regiment and division were headed again toward Bull Run and left only a few companies on guard. He didn't know that Gen. James Shields and his division of 7,000 were four miles away. He was surprised when Shields forced him up the valley. A nice victory for us.

"Maybe we can take the measure of this Stonewall."

Charley wrote from his tent, where he could see the Columbia Furnace iron works on the banks of Big Stony Creek.

"Details from our company and Company F went on an all-night march with some of the boys from Pennsylvania, Indiana and New York, right into Secesh ranks at Hudson's Corners near here. We captured fifty-nine cavalry troops, horses, weapons and stores from Ashby's Cavalry Regiment. But Jackson's men got even, taking Winchester again and pushing us back sixty-five miles.

"In thirty-six hours of grueling fighting, we lost one man. Some were wounded and more than fifty captured. So far we've been in Winchester four times, and I wouldn't care to visit again.

"I have a feeling we'll see Jackson a few more times before this rebellion is quelled."

He re-read the last letter from home. "Yes, the Battle of Shiloh was bloody, but old Gen. Ulysses S. Grant turned that Confederate surprise attack into a Union win," he wrote. "And how about Adm. David Farragut's capture of the Port of New Orleans? We Connecticut sons are gloating that the admiral's ship, the *U.S.S. Hartford*, was named for the capital of our state!"

He heard the call for mail and hurried to finish.

"Thanks for the food package. It was much appreciated by all. Next time, can you also send some roasted coffee beans? Uncle Sam issues us raw beans that we roast ourselves over the campfire. It would be nice to celebrate my eighteenth birthday with some good strong, real, coffee beans from home.

"By the way, we're now part of the First Brigade, First Division, Second Army Corps, of the new Army of Virginia, under Gen. John Pope. Sounds confusing, since Gen. Stonewall Jackson heads the Valley District of the Army of Northern Virginia, under Gen. Lee. Definitely not the same army."

He quickly sealed the envelope, marked it "postage due" and dropped the letter into the mailbag. He sauntered over to the sutler's wagon and met up with Oliver and another volunteer, Lew Johnson.

Lew was arguing with Oliver while the sutler, Henry Davis, looked on with an amused smile.

"Oliver, just lend me a dollar," Lew said urgently. "I'll have enough then for the whiskey. I'll pay you back."

"You said that last month," Oliver said glumly.

Lew turned to Charley. "Have a dollar to spare?"

Charley shook his head. "I'm close to my limit. The sutler has most of my pay from last time." He looked sideways at Davis, who appeared not to hear.

Lew turned his full attention to Charley. "A shot of whiskey will comfort you quicker than writing a letter."

"I'll lend you fifty cents. Maybe you can borrow the rest from someone else."

Lew took the coins and looked hopefully at Oliver, who shook his head. Lew moved off to the tents.

Charley said to Davis, "I'll take tobacco, if it's not stale."

"My merchandise is absolutely fresh," the sutler said with a smile. He put down his newspaper and handed over the tobacco.

Smoking cigarettes was one Southern custom Charley enjoyed learning. They beat the cigars back home. He tapped tobacco into a rolling paper, twisted it closed and lit up.

"Anything about the war?" he asked, gesturing to the newspaper. His family didn't need to read more bad news about losses.

"A couple of complications," the sutler said. "You know that the English and French have sided with the Secessionist states?"

Charley nodded. "Something about the Confederacy being its own nation."

"It didn't help that we had to free those two Rebel commissioners headed for England and

France on that British mail steamer, *The Trent*, last fall," Oliver said. "I think Capt. Wilkes was right to board the ship and take those men to prison. They were traitors."

"Yeah, but Lincoln backed off when the Brits sent 11,000 troops to Canada and threatened to attack us for stopping their ship on the high seas," Davis said. "That was a close call."

Charley blew out a puff of smoke with a forceful grunt. "They should let us do our job of putting down these Rebels without interfering. They just want their foot back in the door."

The sutler nodded. "The Brits say the southern states are strong enough to be their own country, and have proven their right to separate from Lincoln's government. They've offered to step in and mediate the issues between the North and South. Another way of saying they would give the South what it wants."

Charley scoffed. "They see what they want to see. They conveniently forget we captured Fort Henry, or the port at New Orleans or Memphis. Or sent the Rebs running at Shiloh. And no matter what anyone says, the South didn't win at Seven Pines."

Oliver moved away and Charley followed. "Those all were yesterday," Oliver said, with a wave of his hand. "We'll win the others. We were just practicing before."

They headed for the ball field. "Let's see if they need us for today's game," Charley said.

Oliver nodded. "Wish Lew was in good enough shape to play. He's a really strong hitter when he's sober."

"Whiskey is trouble for him," Charley said. "He's already half drunk sometimes when we begin a march. I don't see how he can stay on his feet. But he's not the only one. And the sutler knows the sale of alcohol was banned two months ago."

"You're thinking he should turn scrupulous? Besides, the officers get a whiskey ration, and so do we, sometimes. Just not from him." They turned their attention to the two team captains choosing up sides.

By June, Charley's regiment and the rest of the Second Corps of the Army of Virginia were on the march again into Stonewall's territory. They tramped sixty-two miles south through the valley to Front Royal, Virginia, then headed further south a few days later.

7
Cedar Mountain

The Corps marched twenty-four miles to Luray, scouting ahead for signs of the enemy. The rumor was they were headed either for Richmond or Bull Run for a second try at victory.

"Jackson again," Charley said grimly when they passed east of the Rebel-held Winchester.

"He got the better of us most of the Spring," Oliver said. "He's earned his name, Stonewall.

In blistering August heat, they crossed the Blue Ridge range to Warrenton and turned south, passing through a series of small villages. Charley looked down into the picturesque valleys and across the high blue ridges. The terrain of rolling hills and lush farms was majestic.

If only the people at home could see what he was seeing. But would this make his father even more certain he was on a lark? He shook his head.

To the rear, the army of thousands wound around rough mountain terrain for as far as he could see. He thrilled to the show of might, although many marchers stopped to rest along the wayside in the punishing heat.

He shifted his haversack on his aching shoulders. Fifty pounds of blankets, clothes, food and tent were taking their toll. He focused on one step at a time, until they halted for a rest break. Soon the smell of steaming coffee ran up the lines of the groups of men crouching together over small fires fueled by roadside brush.

Wearily, Charley took off his boots. He lost count of how many pairs he wore out.

"A week old, and I can put my fingers through the holes," he complained to Oliver. He unrolled his rubber blanket. It kept him dry when they slept outdoors, but now he had a more immediate need. He used his knife to hack a couple of pieces off one end, trimming them roughly to the shape of the soles. He put the boots back on and walked up and down by the campfire, testing them.

All down the line, men tossed away jackets and other clothing to lighten their loads.

Oliver emptied half his knapsack onto the ground. He rearranged his cooking utensils, canteen, and family letters.

"That should do it," he said. "By the time I'll need a coat and half this stuff, we'll have new supplies anyway."

He pulled hardtack from his knapsack, dunked it in his coffee and waited.

"Buggy as last week's," he said, poking at the squirmers on the surface of the three-inch square. He skimmed off the insects and settled down to munch the softened cracker and sip the hot and strong brew.

Too soon, the drummer sounded the beat to get back into formation, and they were on the road again. They halted just south of Culpeper. Charley's brigade, under Gen. Samuel Crawford, was the only infantry to reach the destination. The brigade set up tents in the fields, cooked the evening meal, tended to their muskets, and rested, while they waited for the rest of the troops to catch up.

In the dusk, Charley heard a suspicious noise and squinted toward the horizon. Others did the same.

"We're not alone," he said. He could make out movement of horses and wagons over the wheat field in front of them. Not where friendly forces would be.

He scanned past the sheaves left standing to dry. "No mistake. They know we're here."

His heartbeat quickened. The brigade was isolated. It was a perfect setup for an attack.

Charley drew picket duty that night. From his post, he could hear Union troops in the far distance, heading their way. But Confederate artillery and wagons were already rumbling into position, right opposite. He could see the shadows through the dim starlight and hear the muffled voices.

At the light of day, they had their first clear view of the field. Facing them was a long enemy line, in position, directly ahead.

Scattered artillery shots broke out. The brigade returned fire. Shots continued through the morning. Infantry units shifted their battle positions.

Gen. Crawford moved the men a mile to the right in a section of woods, still facing the wheat field. Fifth Connecticut was up front, with the Twenty-eighth New York and Forty-sixth Pennsylvania. The Tenth Maine Regiment was to the left.

Cedar Mountain, to the south, was a somber witness over the golden fields.

About five o'clock, Lieut. Col. George Chapman, the regiment's commanding officer, passed along the rear.

"Men, this is our first real fight of the war. It's almost time," he said quietly. "Remember you're representing Connecticut. Don't disgrace her."

Charley thought back to Bull Run. The colonel's message was clear. He fidgeted and rechecked his musket. Loaded and ready. He glanced at Oliver, grim and watchful.

The order came to remove the high rail fence in front of them.

The order came to charge.

Charley trained his eyes on the woods at the far end of the field as they raced across and down a slope that formed the bank of a small brook.

Suddenly gunfire erupted directly in front of them. The Rebels had been waiting, unseen, flat on the ground behind a fence on the far side of the brook.

The first volley mercilessly mowed down the Union front line. Elijah, the Color Sergeant, crumbled, and another man grabbed the flag before it could hit the ground.

Oliver fell. So did Owen.

Charley kept his eyes and his musket trained ahead, but a panicky voice inside told him what just happened.

The artillery and muskets on both sides pounded away. Gunsmoke shrouded the battlefield. The two forces closed in on each other. Angry enemy faces within an arm's reach filled his line of sight. The Corps pressed the enemy back from the fence, through the woods and into the open fields beyond the trees.

The Rebels seemed caught by surprise, and their greater numbers yielded to the smaller Union force that attacked the weakness along the Rebels' left flank and began to roll up the entire line.

Until, out of the Confederate line, there came an astonishing sight: A general, riding swiftly to the front, waving a sword and scabbard in one hand and the Confederate battle flag in the other, yelling a rallying cry.

Stonewall Jackson.

His men roared in answer. Transformed, they surged into the Union troops. Enemy reinforcements appeared, and the Union brigade was nearly surrounded. Massive numbers were captured, including Col. Chapman. Casualties, dead or mortally wounded, covered the ground.

When the firing ceased, Union survivors fell back a short distance. A quick count showed a hundred men were captured, another hundred were wounded. Forty-eight were killed or mortally wounded. Of the one hundred men of Charley's regiment that morning, only eight were left standing. They re-formed under Capt. Henry Daboll of Company H, and were kept in reserve.

Charley's pain and confusion turned to disbelief when Gen. Franz Sigel loudly arrived after dark, marching onto the field with bugles blowing and drums beating. The Rebels immediately opened fire.

The music stopped abruptly. In the uproar, the general's pack mules, horses, cooks and servants were mowed down.

"Stupid, stupid, stupid," Charley muttered.

Gen. Banks requested a truce so the men still standing could safely attempt recovery and rescue of the dead and wounded. It began at dawn Sunday, even as scattered skirmishing continued.

The battlefield sight was horrific. Thousands of bodies were piled everywhere in the unrelenting heat. Most of the dead were already badly swollen and dissolving. Charley couldn't believe such horror could happen so quickly. The men burying the dead hardly recognized anyone.

Charley found Oliver near Elijah's and Owen's crumbled bodies.

He dropped to his knees. "Oliver," he choked. "We were supposed to go home together." He bent over the disfigured body in anguish.

Two days later, the Union troops watched Gen. Lee's army disappear over the hills in the distance. Gen. Pope pulled the federal troops back and sent the baggage teams to Alexandria. Stonewall's forces passed around Pope's flank and got to the rear, destroying Union supply lines and capturing railcars filled with food and weapons at Manassas Junction.

Charley wrote home.

"Stonewall Jackson defeated us in the first hard battle the Fifth Connecticut was engaged in," he said. "Oliver is gone, Elijah and Owen are gone. They were three of our best men, and the first from our city to give their lives in battle in this war for the land they loved.

"There is a great deal of suffering among the rest of us. There have been several days where we've had nothing to eat. The men are very despondent, and several have deserted."

He put down his pencil and bowed his head.

Not a lark, Dad.

8
Hunger and Bloodshed

Nearly half the three hundred and eighty men and boys of the Fifth were killed, wounded or captured at Cedar Mountain. All told, the Twelfth Corps suffered more than three hundred dead, 1,300 wounded and nearly six hundred missing. More than a third of the two divisions was gone.

The numbers were beyond anything Charley could have imagined. And inside those figures was the loss of his closest friends. Only he and seven other members of the regiment still stood. The stunned Second Corps was pulled out of battle ranks and out of Culpeper, and fell back toward Washington.

On retreat they were ordered to protect eight stranded Union railcars containing rations and supplies that the Rebels had not destroyed at Manassas Junction. The cars could not be moved to safety—the Rebels had burned the bridges to the Union rear.

All the while Charley stood guard, he could hear the raging battle at Bull Run, three miles away. In the end, with no promise of other rations, the hungry troops of the Corps were ordered to burn the supply cars to keep them out of enemy hands.

Then they swung south of the Orange & Alexandria Railroad and east some eighty miles to meet up with the rest of the army at Bentonville, Virginia. Stonewall was in this battle too, but the Rebels' Maj. Gen. Longstreet was the man who led 25,000 men in a massive assault against Gen. Pope. At least the determined Union rear guard prevented a complete rout.

Charley's hunger was desperate. Once they settled in camp he walked back a mile to scour out cracker crumbs from nearly empty boxes of rations he had seen earlier on the side of the road.

The next day, near Chantilly, pounded by gunfire in a raging thunderstorm, the Confederates again tried to get to the Yanks' rear and surround the troops. Union commanders Brig. Gen. Isaac Stevens and Maj. Gen. Philip Kearny were killed. Pope's men headed for Fairfax in the morning. The

Corps, still on guard duty, marched the eleven miles to Alexandria and camped near Fort Richardson.

The men learned that several companies of the First Connecticut Heavy Artillery were camped at the fort, and they went looking for familiar faces.

Charley met up with Norwalker Pvt. Gould Saunders.

"Charley! Good grief, man, are you OK?"

"Later, Gould. First, do you have any food to spare?"

Gould led him to his cook fire and poured him coffee. He gave him meat and bread. Charley wolfed down the food and described what the men of the Corps lived through the last few days. Reluctantly, he finally stood up.

"Time to get back, Gould. Thanks for saving a starving soldier."

The Corps received new orders and were attached to the First Brigade, First Division, Twelfth Army Corps of the Army of the Potomac, under Maj. Gen. McClellan.

Three days later, Sept. 17, 1862, the Twelfth headed toward Sharpsburg, Maryland, which the Union forces called Antietam, to head off Gen. Lee and his Army of Northern Virginia in an attempt to invade the North for the first time.

71

Charley's regiment and the Twenty-ninth Ohio were detached from the Corps at Frederick, where the Southern forces had camped only hours before. Charley pulled guard duty with the detached units, while the rest of the Corps chased along the twenty miles to their destination.

He waited tensely for news of the battle, sometimes imagining bloody scenes in flashbacks of Cedar Mountain. The reality was even worse. The armies clashed head-on for twelve hours on a farmer's fields. In the end, neither side could declare a clear victory. Gen. Lee pulled his depleted army back across the Potomac the night of September 18.

Union casualties told a grim story. Charley stood guard at one of the two hospital camps outside town and dully watched the parade of ambulances and wagons carry the screaming, moaning or unconscious wounded into Frederick. The tented camps quickly filled with over 1,000 wounded each. Yet casualties kept arriving, and every church and public building became a hospital for an additional 7,000, some near death.

On the battlefield, Union soldiers dug graves for over a week, burying dead of both sides.

Gen. Joseph Mansfield, Charley's Corps commander, was among those killed.

A week later, Charley stopped by Henry Davis's wagon. The sutler said the northern papers called the battle a Union victory because it kept

Gen. Lee from advancing into Maryland. Charley read the numbers: Union dead, wounded, mortally wounded, missing or captured were 12,400 out of 75,316 men. The Confederate casualties were 10,700 out of 51,844.

"They call this a victory," Charley said softly. "It was a slaughter. We lost more men than they did."

"That's not how Washington is thinking," Davis said. "The Rebels lost a fifth of their army. The President is pressing to have the Confederates settle this war and come back into the fold.

"Look at this news dispatch. President Lincoln released a draft of an Emancipation Proclamation, to make all slaves free in the South, and to welcome the rebellious states back into the Union by January."

Charley shook his head. "The Secesh say the Confederate States of America are a separate country, with their own constitution. From what we've seen here, they don't mean to change that."

The sutler shrugged. "This document sure has gotten all sides talking up a storm. The Abolitionists are praising the President, supporters of the Confederation are condemning him to hell, and the blacks in the North are holding celebrations.

"Some newspapers say the proclamation's a daring ploy to keep the French and English out of the war. After all, they abolished slavery years ago.

How would it look if they backed a government that supports slavery?"

Charley grew thoughtful.

"That would mean… This is now officially a war mostly about slavery? More than about patriotism, about reuniting the country?"

"Some would say it always was," the sutler said.

Meanwhile, back in Bear Creek, Marse stormed into the kitchen where I was clearing ashes from the woodburning stove. I backed away fast when Marse stuffed in a newspaper. He didn't even notice the stove was cold. He stalked out and called loudly for the Missus.

I grabbed the paper and ran to the barn.

"Cato, quick. Marse was so mad about something he read that he didn't see the stove wasn't lit. Can you help me make out what it says?"

They climbed quickly into the hayloft to be out of Marse's sight. Cato read and began to laugh.

"Hallelujah! I never thought this day would come. It's official, Jimmy John, the President wants to make us free. Slaves no more, sold no more!"

I took the newspaper and tried to reason out the article through the few words I could recognize.

Cato pointed to words over my shoulder. "First, he's giving the Confederate states a chance to join the Union again. After January 1, though, we'll be free—unless something else happens."

He was suddenly silent.

"That 'something else' could be if the South wins this war, of course," he said finally.

My heart pounded for so many things, I didn't know which affected me most.

Cato said free. But then he said the South could win. And I could hear Marse raging through the barnyard with that whip again.

9
Winter 1862-63

Charley couldn't shake his gloom. The disasters at Cedar Mountain and Antietam left their mark. He went to roll call, drilled, followed orders. And tried not to think.

Never again could he joke with Oliver or Elijah or Owen about the bad coffee or the giant blister on his heel or the officer who overslept that morning. Like the others in the company he was hungry, ragged, despondent, mourning, always on the alert for attacks.

At roll call every morning there were other names called out that didn't answer. Deserters.

The lieutenant assigned guards to stop desert-ers from leaving. It was unnerving, guarding against their own brothers. Yet, when Charley was part of a detail to bring four hundred Rebel prisoners to Fort McHenry in Baltimore, one of the detail itself con-fided he was leaving.

"Man, think about what you're saying," Char-ley said. "Remember, you and I volunteered to give three years to the Union army. No one forced us to sign up."

The soldier laughed, shaking his head.

"That's high and mighty talk. We didn't sign up to be starved and to freeze and to march up and down this country, and to fight to the death or re-treat. We don't even get pay for months on end. I say we have a right to quit."

Charley said quietly, "You desert and you can never go back home. Not just for your family. Just about everyone in town has someone in this war. It's not right, letting them, or us, down."

The soldier turned away. Charley watched him and three other guards talk in low whispers. He was now the outsider. He sensed their discussion would not end well. Yet he didn't have the heart to turn them in.

He desperately wanted to go home, and forget about all this. It was a powerful feeling, something he wouldn't admit to his father. Still, deserting would not mean freedom, and he couldn't leave his brothers that way.

Meanwhile, Union survivors captured at Cedar Mountain were released in an exchange with Rebels and returned to the regiment. There were many ill and wounded among them. Plans were made to send them home, as well as the ailing men in the field hospital, including Charles Beers, his bunkmate since Oliver died, and the friend who helped him volunteer in the first place. He was due to be discharged from the Army by the end of the year.

"Beers," Charley said. "I'll see you on my next furlough, whenever that is. Write and let me know how things are going. I know my folks are worried and maybe they aren't telling me everything going on there."

Beers waved with a weak smile as the wagon pulled away. Charley stepped back. He thought about his own bout with typhoid and was grateful he survived to rejoin the fight. Too many men were losing their lives in this war by illness.

A couple of days later, the Corps moved south to Fairfax Station to meet up with recruits arriving on the Orange and Alexandria Railroad. Charley spotted a Norwalk neighbor, William Jennings, among them.

"Will, welcome to the war." Charley shook his hand.

Will looked happy to see him but after a few minutes he admitted he almost hadn't recognized him. "You've changed," he said. "You look older. Thinner."

"Yeah," Charley said. "I'm always hungry. Older is a little trickier. Like you, I'm eighteen. I was sixteen when I joined up. Today, a year and a half later, I'm twenty-one, if you look the dates on my enlistment papers."

Two other neighbors, Ted Baldwin and Jim Scranton, were among the new recruits. Right away, the four agreed to share a tent. Charley felt a little better seeing fresh and healthy faces from home.

He tried not to think about the four deserters, but a few days later he spotted them in the custody of the Cavalry Patrol.

Christmas passed, and so did the new year, and homesickness hung heavy over the camp. The boys got packages from home and hungrily read the letters.

January 1863 was no friendlier than December 1862. The weather was cold, rainy and blustery on the regiment's march to rejoin the brigade and the Twelfth Corps. Tents blew down and blankets and clothing got soaked. They tried to warm up at their cooking fires, but the wood was too green to give off much heat. Rations were mostly hardtack and coffee and questionable beef.

Still, they managed to shake off their gloom for a few hours now and then. At night they consoled themselves with songs around the fire, traded jokes and stories, played cards, and looked for other ways to kill the boredom and forget their miseries.

Morale plummeted for the newest recruits, who expected to fight Rebels, not struggle against Mother Nature.

Meanwhile, the Twelfth Corps did not participate in the bloodbath at Fredericksburg. Gen. Stonewall Jackson teamed with Gen. James Longstreet in a two-day struggle that drove Union Gen. Ambrose Burnside back across the Potomac River once more.

Instead, the Twelfth marched toward Stafford Court House, slogging through endless rain. They struggled to move wagons that sank to their axles in mud. Cannons riding on caissons disappeared up to their muzzles.

They arrived at the town, little more than the court house building itself, to guard the logistical and transportation center. At least there were log houses built by the Ohio regiment formerly stationed there.

They were dry and warm, even those in the four-man tents, in spite of the cold and the change from constant rain to great drifts of snow. Other conditions became more tolerable.

Gen. "Fighting Joe" Hooker replaced Gen. Burnside as head of the Army of the Potomac.

"This is the fifth general President Lincoln has appointed in these two years of war," Charley grumbled as he set up yet another pot of coffee. "At least this general makes these long hours of guard duty more bearable. Rations are better. Clothing is warmer."

The troops also received new recognition.

The general ordered badges for each corps. The Twelfth was given stars—red for the first division, white for the second, and blue for the third. The men of the Fifth Regiment were in the first brigade, first division.

"Stars. We're the stars," Charley joked as he sewed his red star to his cap. "Besides, the badges will make it easier to see who's slacking off and who's getting the job done."

"Remember to hide the cap, then, when our luck is down," Will warned.

Charley, Will, Ted and Jim were assigned to a 300-man detail to hack down trees and lay the trunks crossways to build a corduroy road over the mud. The road connected their camp to the Eleventh Corps camp at Brook's Station, a mile away. They stretched out the heavy work for a full month to avoid guard duty. It didn't hurt that they were given a ration of whiskey every afternoon as a bonus.

They also found plenty of distractions.

There was the time a local enterprising pedlar approached in a two-horse wagon loaded with peach pies to sell. Those pies sure looked good, but no one had any money.

"Raid!" a soldier called out, and the men leaped to their feet. The alarmed pedlar tried to flee. A front wheel on his wagon hit a stump. The harness snapped. The pies mysteriously vanished before he could get back on the road.

A few days later, the restless men of Company B eyed a sutler's store situated at the top of the hill above them. "He just had a big delivery. He's got to have more than writing paper," one speculated.

Stealthily, after dark, they surrounded the store and spotted a barrel of beer stored inside. Whispering and laughing and shushing each other, they rolled it quickly into camp and partied all night. At morning roll call, the sergeant demanded that the culprits own up, but the men shook their heads and acted innocent. No one could prove a thing.

Charley overheard some officers saying they thought morale had improved somehow.

Nature still gave them grief. Heavy snow again gave way to rain and deep mud.

This kind of mud couldn't happen in Connecticut, Charley cussed, as the boys in the detail put their shoulders against wagons to move the supplies and ammunition that the mules could not. Farmers back home complained about the rocky soil—this muck was a lot worse.

The hours were long and the duty hard into spring. But the terrors of earlier battles faded. The men were getting rested and strong, and anxious to move on.

Finally, the last week of April they were told to prepare to break camp for an advance—again, "somewhere." Grateful, Charley cleaned his spotless musket, checked his ammunition, and brushed off his cap with its new star.

10
Chancellorsville

"This looks like a big one," Charley said as they crammed their haversacks with seven days' food rations and a hundred rounds of ammunition. He was glad to be moving on, even though Cedar Mountain taught him not to underestimate the enemy. Not in whatever this battle was, or the next one. Or the next.

"All seven corps are moving out. Maybe we're heading for Richmond," Will said.

Charley grunted. "Or Fredericksburg, where Lee's holing up."

At sunrise on Monday, April 27, Maj. Gen. Henry W. Slocum's 46,000-man force of cavalry, infantry and artillery headed northwest toward the Rappahannock River. They were mentally ready for action, singing and passing jokes up and down the ranks of the brigade.

Anything could get the wisecracks started, from Jim's sneezing fit over pollen floating from the trees to Ted's cheerful warning that this particular batch of hardtack was guaranteed to make them toothless.

They tented for the night at Kelly's Ford. In the morning they crossed the Rapahannock over pontoon bridges and turned south. Soon enough, the advance troops met up with Rebels and captured two hundred men stationed at the Elys Ford riverfront. They faced almost no opposition after that. A good sign.

The army continued on to the Rapidan River. The brigade's engineers used axes, saws and hammers to build a temporary bridge over the river for the supply wagons, and the men up front braced themselves to ford the waist-deep water. The air was warm, the river was frigid.

They shed pants and shoes and hoisted them on their muskets, held high to keep them dry. Some men hauled ammunition that had been on the backs of mules floundering on the banks. Hollering and cussing, the men pushed through the deep and rocky river, and hurried back into their uniforms on the other side.

The engineers completed the bridge in two hours for the wagons, and the rest of the mules and the men of the Second Division and the Eleventh Corps.

The troops clearly were in Rebel territory now. They turned back a cavalry attack and by the afternoon they arrived at their destination, a brick mansion and tavern owned by a family named Chancellor, on the crossroads of the turnpike and Plank Road.

Gen. Hooker made the house his headquarters.

They were south of Fredericksburg, well in the rear of Lee's army, and eleven miles north of Richmond, blocking the Rebel army from the secessionist capital and supply base.

Charley looked around the rolling open fields, the swampland, and dense shrubbery. "Like so many other places we've been, Chancellorsville doesn't look much like a town," he said.

"It's a good location," Will said. "The roads from here go to all parts of Virginia. Gen. Hooker has laid down the challenge to Lee. We're rested and ready for him."

The troops settled in. The next morning, Friday, they were sweltering from the rising heat but ready, waiting for orders from the confident officers.

Charley wondered about that heavy shrubbery just ahead. An officer said an iron ore furnace was located in the area around the time of the American Revolution, and most of the large trees back then had been cut down for fuel. The troops were now facing a mile-long, twisted mess of brush, small evergreens and vines they could hardly see through.

Heavy Rebel artillery opened up early from the direction of Fredericksburg. The Corps built a long chest-high barrier of stones, branches and dirt called breastworks and waited behind it. Before the day ended they could see enemy lines forming along their front.

Early Saturday, Charley and Will watched a dust cloud moving to their right along the road from Richmond.

"Only thing I know that would raise a slow and steady cloud like that is troops," Charley said. "Given the direction they're marching, it looks like they're in retreat."

Will laughed. "They gave up so quick?"

They kept watching. About four o'clock, the commander moved the division in front of the breastworks to intercept that army.

Charley was uneasy that no guard remained to protect the defenses they had taken the trouble to put in place the day before.

The men studied the thousands of enemy in butternut and gray uniforms rapidly marching past, and into the thick woods.

Charley froze. "Stonewall," he said, looking at the flags.

Then, urgently, to Will, "Look. He's not retreating, he's up to his old game. He's moving around our entire front, right at the Eleventh Corps. His forces must have split from Lee's to flank us." Murmurs along the line showed the officers and the other boys also figured out the Rebel strategy.

The division was ordered to skirmish with the Rebels protecting the flanks of the main body of their marching army. The division pressed through the swamp after the enemy for nearly a mile.

At dusk, the Twelfth was ordered to fall back to the breastworks. They scrambled in the growing darkness back through the swamp, turning and firing as Rebel skirmishers pursued them. Heavy Rebel artillery and musket fire began thundering near where the 8,000 men of the Eleventh had been positioned. Half of that Corps was captured without firing a shot.

The Rebel roar continued, closing fast along Plank Road, coming right at the Twelfth. Remaining soldiers of the Eleventh raced to the Twelfth's breastworks, with the Rebels on their tail. Rebels and Yanks turned left and tangled in murderous confusion.

Charley's regiment turned to the right behind the defenses, evading the enemy and setting up firing positions to hold the center and the right flank in support of the New Jersey Brigade of the Third Corps under Gen. Daniel Sickels. A division of the Second Corps swelled the defenders at the breastworks to 37,000 men.

Still, the Rebels poured in relentlessly. Stonewall's men captured twenty-one men of the Fifth Regiment, including the commander, Col. Warren Packer. The intense shooting ignited fires in the tangled and smoky undergrowth in front of them. Trapped and wounded soldiers screamed helplessly in the flames.

Inhuman Rebel yells shattered the night air. Guns on both sides pounded relentlessly through the smoke and shouts and cries of pain. Charley and the others of the Fifth continued firing at shadows that loomed through the smoke.

As day broke Sunday, the exhausted regiment was moved to the rear and its position was taken over by the Twentieth Connecticut. Casualties mounted as both sides fought to unite their divided armies. In the end, the much larger Union forces were the first to retreat.

The toll was hellish. Nearly 195,000 men had clashed, with over 17,000 Union and nearly 13,000 Confederate casualties. Charley's regiment lost some sixty men, including those who were captured.

That night, Charley tried to absorb what had happened.

Union regiments were unable to reclaim their defenses. Men confident in the beginning that they had the upper hand against the much smaller Rebel force were captured. Some Union forces were never called into battle and the men who were called were ordered to pull back, often when they felt they had the advantage.

Charley watched and obeyed, in disbelief and humiliation. It was Cedar Mountain all over again, only worse. Stonewall had fooled them again. And time after time, their own Gen. Hooker failed to act on the offensive.

At roll call, the weary colonel tried to cheer the men with the news that while the South won this battle, it suffered a grave setback—Gen. Stonewall Jackson himself was a casualty.

The word spread quickly that Gen. Jackson and Maj. Gen. A. P. Hill went on a reconnaissance of the battlefield about 9 p.m. Saturday. North Carolina soldiers, mistaking the group for Yanks, opened fire, and two bullets hit Jackson in his left arm and his right hand. Gen. Hill was struck by a Union shell. Both were quickly moved from the battlefield. Doctors amputated Stonewall's arm.

For Charley, the Union loss to a force half their size, and the failure to take advantage of many chances to strike on the battlefield, and Gen.

Hooker's puzzling advances and withdrawals, was more than frustrating. This had been their battle to win. Instead, the victory went to Gen. Lee for his masterful strategy and tactics.

Charley and Will talked quietly out of the ear-shot of their officers. "We have no one on our side with the same courage and cleverness of a Jackson or a Lee," Will said.

Charley seethed. "Our leaders failed us."

Charley later wrote home, "This is not just a private's opinion, but the opinion of thousands of our army, that it was not the soldiers of the Army of the Potomac that were defeated, but rather the officers who commanded the army. It was a campaign of worse than blunders."

By Tuesday, May 5, the regiment settled at its old camp at Stafford Court House. A week later the men learned that Stonewall Jackson was dead, not of complications from the amputation, but from pneumonia.

"He was against us in every engagement since we came South two years ago," Will reflected. "We watched him urging on his tough, disciplined men in battle, with no apparent concern for his own safety. I wonder if they have any more like him to bedevil us."

Col. Packer was paroled and exchanged by the Rebels in June, and once again the Corps packed up and headed on the road, burning for a victory, and soon.

"Hell, we're darned sight better soldiers than when we got down here a year and a half ago," Charley stormed. "We just need the chance to show what we can do."

Letters from home worsened his mood. Folks repeatedly questioned why the war was still dragging on after two years. Charley read his father's letters, pushing for an end to the war, maybe by treaty. It made no sense, he wrote, that their men and boys were mowed down by the thousands in this foolish war when they should be at home.

This was not just what he thought, he said, but the growing feeling of neighbors and friends.

Charley ached to make his father understand. He did not want to go home by concession or an agreement on paper. And not by shame. Around him, disgusted and disillusioned men continued to desert. Charley didn't even try to argue with them. He had a score to settle for Oliver and Elijah and Owen. And for all those lost at Chancellorsville.

A month later, he witnessed the price of desertion, at Leesburg, Virginia, thirty miles outside Washington D.C.

On June 18, the Corps was ordered to form an open square in a large field. Three deserters, two from Pennsylvania and one from a New Jersey regiment, sat on open coffins in the center, next to newly dug graves.

Firing squads, three details of twelve soldiers each, faced them. On command the details fired, and the deserters crumbled backwards into their plain pine boxes. They were the first to be executed in the Army of the Potomac. The entire division of 6,000 men then was solemnly marched past the coffins.

Charley wondered whether the men he tried to talk out of leaving six months earlier at Frederick, Virginia, would meet the same end.

11
Gettysburg

The Corps moved out of Virginia and into a section of Maryland where they had spent nearly the whole first year of their enlistment. By June 28 they were in Frederick City. Gen. Lee was somewhere ahead. The Rebels had retaken Winchester, crossed Maryland, and entered Pennsylvania.

Word was, the Southern general, riding on the success at Chancellorsville, felt it was time to again try to bring the war north. The rich Pennsylvania farmlands could feed his tattered and hungry army. He allowed his men to take federal supplies where they found them, but he forbid them from stealing private property. The soldiers paid shopkeepers for food with Confederate money, worthless in the northern states.

The gloom running through the Corps was that if Lee could capture the state capital, Harrisburg, he could force the Union to sue for peace. Charley burned to tangle again with the Rebs and show the North could win. The trouble was their leader, Gen. Hooker. He had taken good care of them over a hard winter, but Charley could not forget Chancellorsville.

Hooker might not have been able to forget that battle, either. As soon as they reached Frederick City, he asked to be relieved as commander. The President immediately named Gen. George Meade to replace him. Meade also fought at Chancellorsville but Charley didn't know much about him, other than a rumor that he really didn't want this job.

"Great," he said, shaking his head. "Just what we need."

At least Meade did not wait to act. He immediately went tracking Lee's army, scattered over central Pennsylvania. Two days later, the Twelfth Corps moved through hot and nearly windless weather to the southern Pennsylvania border town of Littlestown. Other Union troops were already in the state near the college town of Gettysburg, a hub of main roads and railroads leading in all directions. More troops were on the way.

On Wednesday, July 1, Charley's regiment and the rest of the Twelfth, made up of men from Connecticut, Maryland and Pennsylvania, were on the road at seven o'clock in the morning, marching towards Gettysburg. The cavalry went on ahead, hunting out the enemy.

Gen. Lee's armies were streaming in from Chambersburg and Cashtown in the west, and from the Susquehanna River to the northeast.

Charley could feel and hear the heavy thump of artillery pounding from the town and see and smell the rolling clouds of gunsmoke long before reaching Gettysburg. The First Corps and the Eleventh were heavily engaged to the west and north when they arrived about four o'clock.

The air was oppressive, almost as though Nature itself was holding its breath over what was to come next.

Four Union corps and two cavalry units poured in from as far east and south as Emmitsburg, Maryland. Relieved townspeople welcomed them with food, water and thanks as they marched quickly through the streets. By the end of the day, 94,000 Union troops and 72,000 Rebels had crowded in, positioning themselves in the streets and the craggy ridges surrounding the town.

Charley could see the battle was not going well in town. Confederates retreated from the streets when the Union soldiers pressed through, but then came roaring back. Yanks were chased through a gauntlet, the enemy firing at them from the left and right. The brigade lost half its men. Even Gen. John Reynolds was killed.

The Twelfth was sent to the extreme right of the army and settled in for the night at the foot of Culp's Hill. They were thirsty and their canteens were empty. Luckily, it didn't take long to discover that they were near Spangler's Spring, a source of abundant cool and pure underground water. The men crowded around and drank deeply. They filled their canteens. And waited.

That night Charley drifted in and out of a restless sleep, until the sky began to lighten, revealing the landscape in dark silhouette. Birds started their early calls back and forth just as the morning drum call sounded insistently. Four a.m. sure came fast. The men hustled into position on the hill and built breastworks, using muscle, bayonets and tin plates.

The full Army of the Potomac formed a fish-hook along Cemetery Ridge to Cemetery Hill and east and south to Culp's Hill and the spring. The "hook" protected the army's right flank and allowed Union troops to move inside to reinforce vulnerable spots without exposing themselves to enemy fire. The Twelfth was positioned near the curve, on Culp's. From there, they could also keep an eye on the Union supply line on the Baltimore Pike and as well as the rear of the army on Cemetery Ridge.

Charley settled in to boil coffee and eat the meat he had cooked back in Littlestown. He appraised the landscape before him. Even through the smoke he could see that Gettysburg was a pretty town of homes and businesses, schools, roads and railroads. He looked out over maybe twenty-five square miles, of a wide bowl of boulders, trees, fences and wheat fields surrounded by granite ridges and dotted with more boulders, some tall as a man.

There were plenty of places to hide and shoot from, and plenty where snipers could hide and cut down troops in the open fields below.

"This time we have the higher land," Charley said with satisfaction. "We can't be fooled the way we were at Chancellorsville."

"I've never seen so many Yanks and Johnnies in one place," Will said, squinting through the haze into the bowl and across. "It's like both sides of the whole country's here."

That night, Union men occupied the rocky ridges. Rebels hid in the streets and behind fences in the fields.

The heat rose quickly with the sun. The men waited tensely, peering through the growing smoke and roar at places on the battlefield named Little Round Top, the Wheatfield, Devil's Den and the Peach Orchard.

Two o'clock in the afternoon, the order came to reinforce the Third Corps at Little Round Top. They marched two miles on the double but the call was a false alarm. The Fifth Army Corps got there first and repulsed the enemy.

But Culp's Hill was now vulnerable. The Twelfth hurried back.

Charley and his company went ahead as skirmishers, with orders not to fire any shots, to explore how far the Rebels had advanced. They found out quickly. The Rebels had not only taken over the breastworks, but scores of men in butternut and gray uniforms swarmed around the spring. They let out a yell when they spotted the company and grabbed four men as prisoners.

Charley managed to escape with the rest of the company and report back to the main line. They were ordered to lie down out of sight. And wait. When he could lift his head in the pounding noise and weapons fire, he saw only a mass of blue and butternut in the artillery and musket flashes and smoke.

He tried to shut out the screams of wounded horses and men, the curses and yells of men shooting, and especially from the eerie, high pitched Rebel yells that sounded like a pack of wolves on the kill. The air was filled with the smells of blood, of death, and of the rotting beef in their rations.

It was as near a hell as Charley could imagine, a continuation, magnified, of Cedar Mountain and Chancellorsville. Neither army could budge the other. The Rebels still held the breastworks, but they made no headway toward the crest of the hill.

Charley would learn that this day was the deadliest of the battle.

The Corps' artillery woke up before dawn on the Third. The men battled for seven hours to regain the breastworks. Charley's regiment was sent toward the Baltimore Pike to support an artillery battery stationed behind the main army's position.

The ground trembled under the firing from the guns of the two armies. Gunsmoke blotted out the sun. The weapons-fire flashes were like lightning through the haze. The hill looked like it was on fire.

Two hours later, an immense bombardment by more than a hundred Southern cannons concentrated at the center of the Union line. The Union cannons gave as good as they got. The intensity dug the cannons on both sides into the ground, shifting the angle of the barrels and causing shells to land behind targets.

Anticipating that the Rebel barrage would be followed by an infantry attack, the Union artillery cut back in the afternoon to save ammunition. They waited tensely for the assault. The Rebel storm continued for another hour.

Charley tried to get a sense of developments on the front. He could plainly see only part of the Union line and Maj. Gen. Winfield S. Hancock of the Second Corps, riding along slowly, encouraging the men.

Abruptly, the enemy stopped firing altogether.

An eerie silence followed, except for the sound of marching feet. Then came a blood-curdling Rebel scream from thousands of throats, followed by another furious roar of cannon and musket fire. Shot and shell dropped thick and fast, even around Charley's regiment on guard at the Pike.

They tensed for Rebels coming at them from any angle.

They heard wild cheers from the battlefield.

Thousands of the enemy came running over the ridge, right at them.

"They've broken through the lines," Will shouted.

The regiment braced.

"Will, look!" Charley yelled. "They have no guns!"

Instead, Gen. Hancock's men, rifles ready, were herding Rebels off the field.

Later, some of Hancock's soldiers filled the Fifth in on what had happened. They described how, after the cannon fire ceased, 12,500 Southern soldiers, in formation nearly a mile long and from a mile away, marched relentlessly and silently, bayonets flashing, red flags waving, officers on horseback, from the woods behind Seminary Hill through the sloping corn fields.

The sight was hypnotizing.

The Union men on the front watched in awe as the defiant parade came toward them. The 6,000 Yanks at the center took careful aim and waited until the enemy was in range. Then the artillery, armed with lethal canisters that burst with balls and shrapnel, opened fire. The sides clashed, firing muskets and rifles at point-blank range, stepping over bodies, bayonetting.

Then it was over. Rebels who had not been captured straggled back across the field.

Union soldiers attempted to bring in the wounded on both sides. The sun set on the body-covered field.

Charley heard later that Gen. Lee, Gen. Longstreet and Gen. Pickett led the charge that came to be called Pickett's Charge.

The next day, July 4, Independence Day, was quiet. There was no thought that this was a national holiday, a day when, at home, families got together for picnics and parades. That was a distant world.

The men, exhausted and hungry, heard an occasional rifle shot and tried to cope with the relentless heat. A hard thunder shower in the afternoon worsened the decay of the bodies of men and horses and fresh beef.

The rain finally let up, and the army began the burials. Charley and Will walked along the line of battle. In some places there was no place to step. Blood puddled everywhere. Bodies lay on top of each other. Two batteries had lost nearly every horse. Artillery and ammunition carts were destroyed.

They reached Spangler's Spring. Scores of dead Rebels, some with open canteens in hand, lay in heaps around the spring. Charley guessed they had been killed in the artillery barrage the morning before. He was moved to pity. They had no chance to escape from that rain of fire.

"Poor fellows," he muttered as they turned away.

Charley and Will said little that day, expecting another attack, but none came. On reconnaissance the next morning the regiment found that the enemy retreated during the night toward the Potomac River and Virginia.

The Union Army of the Potomac, filthy, tattered, exhausted and silent, left Gettysburg on Monday, July 6, the way it came, and spent the night in Littlestown. The men rested quietly the next couple of days in sheltering woods, shielded from the blazing sun and the dust rising from the roads.

Then they pushed on to Frederick City, a haul of twenty-eight miles in the steaming weather. The enemy was nowhere to be seen. Charley overheard officers saying quietly that Gen. Meade, as well as he led the army in the battle, was criticized in Washington for failing to attack Lee and his weakened forces before they retreated.

Charley bowed his head. The enemy lost 28,000 men and the Union lost 23,000 in the hardest fighting the country had ever seen. In the Corps' twenty-eight regiments alone, 204 men were killed, 810 were wounded and sixty-seven were missing.

They arrived at camp and he slumped to the ground. Visions of the battle, the bodies, odors of death, the terror, crowded him. Cedar Mountain was a surprise and bloody. Chancellorsville was a nightmare. He had no description yet for Gettysburg. They had won this one, at a terrible price.

Tears streaked down his dirty face, and he could not stop them.

12
Glimmer of Hope

"Deacon Taylor, is this when you and Mr. Hallock met?" Jesse asked. "I thought you was in North Carolina at the time."

I smiled and reminded him, "This is still Charley Hallock's story as he told it to me. He went through a lot, you see, before he got to me. But I can tell you life around the plantation at that time wasn't no quiet time. No suh. It was no quiet time at all.

"Let me tell you more of that before I get back to my friend."

One day about when Charley was marching out of Gettysburg, I remember edging around the verandah where the Missus and the kitchen slaves was shelling peas for dinner. Marse stepped out of the doorway and I dived under the row of holly bushes by the verandah. I cut my foot on the sharp leaves and barely held back a yelp.

Marse sat heavily into the rocker next to the Missus just at that minute. I could hear the rustle of the newspaper.

"Picked up the paper while I was getting the hoof salve for the horse,' he said. "The writer must've poured too much whiskey in his coffee. He says here that Lee's retreating. "That can't be. He had them damn Yankees on the run. At least until Gettysburg. That was just a fluke, a damned fluke."

"Mr. McPherson, watch your language," the Missus warned.

"Well, now, just look at the facts," he said, smacking the newspaper against his leg as he listed each battle.

"In '61, them Yankees retreated like fools after the First Battle of Manassas. In '62 Lee saved Richmond in the Battles of the Seven Days. Stonewall Jackson helped him beat those Yanks in the Second Manassas, and they lost at Fredericksburg.

"In May, we got 'em good at Chancellorsville. Even though we had to lose Stonewall in the bargain. Damned shame, that."

"Mr. McPherson, please. The language! But I agree," the Missus said. "They were lucky when they won at Gettysburg last month. We're not done yet."

She sighed. "If only Gen. Lee had won. Now who knows when this senseless war will end?" She lifted another handful of pods onto her apron.

"Gettysburg,' he mumbled. "A bloody shame."

The Missus stopped shelling.

"'This evil war. It's not as though they don't need cotton for their fancy shirts and soft bed sheets," she said. "They buy from us with one hand and rip out our hearts with the other. All because they don't want us to keep our slaves so's the work can get done."

"Lincoln's almighty Emancipation Proclamation," Marse said sarcastically. He was standing now, pacing dangerously close to where I was crouched under the holly. I shrank back, wincing as new scratches oozed red across my legs.

"Did he seriously think these honorable states that believe in the states' rights under both the federal and the Confederate constitutions would make our slaves free, ruin our economy, just because he said so? Tarnation, he doesn't know what he's saying. And our slaves, if we let them read the newspaper, if they could read at all, don't realize that part of the plan is to bring them into the federal military.

You ask me, when he signed that executive order last January, he wasn't looking to make them free. He was looking to take them for his own plans."

The Missus was quiet at Marse's mention of slaves learning how to read. I risked a peek from my hiding place over at Sara and Addie. They had stopped shelling for a heartbeat and glanced at each other.

Marse leaned over and swatted at Sara. She flinched and jumped back. The wooden bowl slipped from her lap and peas rolled everywhere. Sara scrambled to collect them. By this time Marse was standing over her, whacking her back with the paper.

"What are you doing, wastin' food like that?" he snarled. "Maybe I shouldn't worry about them Yanks taking our food. There won't be any left after you get done throwin' it around."

"Husband, calm yourself. You're gettin' all red in the face, and that ain't good for your blood."

She turned to Sara. "Don't miss a single pea. If I find any you didn't catch, your dinner will be only a dream."

I waited until Marse clomped back into the house, with the Missus and the girls right behind, before I eased myself along the wall and around the corner and made my way to the barn.

The cuts stung. They still was bleeding some. I washed them under the barnyard pump. Somehow, Marse was right behind me again.

Sometimes I felt Marse didn't walk like other folk, you know? Demons carried him on their shoulders, to help him sneak up on a body unawares.

"Jimmy John," he yelled. "Why do I always find you anywhere but where you're supposed to be? I swear to God you're a lazy, useless critter. An auction's coming up next month. I don't know who'd want a lazy runt like you, though."

I waved my hands at Jesse. "So you see things was heating up and getting worse for me on the plantation. I needed to watch and see how to deal with all of this. Things seemed to be getting better for Charley Hallock, though."

In the next weeks the troops of the Twelfth Corps retraced their steps through Frederick, marched past the Antietam battlefield and reached Sandy Hook, Maryland, the place on the Potomac where they had landed two years earlier.

They crossed into Virginia and marched over the mountains of Maryland Heights, Bolivar Heights and Louden Heights in the Blue Ridge range. They continued west toward Manassas Gap on the south side. Gen. Lee and his army kept to the north side of the Shenandoah. The Union army watched the gaps through the mountains to see where the wily Southern general might slip through for a fight.

The Corps reached an old camping ground at the Rappahannock River. They waited there until the mail and supplies caught up with them. Henry Davis set up his wagon store as soon as they settled in. With the mail came the newspapers.

Charley and Will stopped by for tobacco and the sutler's take on the latest events.

"While you were at Gettysburg, four corps under the Army of the Tennessee commanded by Gen. Grant were just as busy in Mississippi," the sutler said. "Look here—Vicksburg fell on July 4. Now the Confederate states are split, divided by the Union's possession of the river."

"That is good news," Charley said. "Maybe our fortunes are turning around. This Grant—what's he like?"

"From what I'm reading, nobody's quite sure. Some say he's a heavy drinker, some took his initials and turned them into the nickname of "Uncondi-tional Surrender" for taking Fort Donelson in Ten-nessee back in '62. The other day there was a dis-patch that said the President couldn't spare him be-cause he was willing to fight."

Charley nodded, hopeful.

The men that night were in good spirits. They reached out to families again, some sending notes home on any paper they could find, including newspaper. The prayer books and card games came out, and when the light grew dim, men took to humming and singing songs from home. Charley and Will smoked some and talked.

"More recruits coming in tomorrow," Will said. "I heard the colonel talking. Most are substitutes for draftees."

"You know they're only here for the money they got from the men who could pay them as substitutes," Charley said. "The last bunch got as much as $1,000 a man, and they gambled and drank it away. Our boys were kept busy guarding them, and almost half deserted anyway."

"You won't be here much longer, will you, Charley?" Will said. "When's your time up?"

"Next year, this time. The thing is, the enlistment papers say I was nineteen at the time. Heck, I'm just nineteen now. This has been a long year."

"The army is pushing for soldiers to re-enlist, even before their time is up," Will said. "What'll you do?"

"Not sure. It would be nice to know I could go home next year, get a normal life back. Signing up for the duration could mean years more trotting around the country, getting shot at. On the other hand, we're getting better with every battle, and I get the feeling these generals are finally getting serious about winning."

Shortly after, the Eleventh and Twelfth Corps were detached from the Army of the Potomac to reinforce troops in Tennessee.

"Looks like we're under Hooker again," Charley said. Images of Chancellorsville flashed through his head. The old anger died hard.

The two corps headed to Brandy Station on the Orange & Alexandria Railroad after turning in their wagons, most of their artillery, and horses.

"Away we went from the grand old Army of the Potomac," Charley wrote home. "We were put on common box freight cars with boards put in for seats for our trip through Washington, Maryland, West Virginia and across the Ohio River. We rode through a large number of cities and towns, where the people came out and cheered for us. They lifted our spirits with fruit and provisions, and finally we arrived in Cowan, Tennessee."

The Eleventh Corps continued on to the battlefront at Chattanooga, while the Twelfth was charged with guarding the twenty-six miles of railroad track between Murfreesboro and Bridgeport. They moved on in a slow, crowded journey through mountains, sleeping nights on the ground, outside the cars.

October came, and the men traveled in open cars. The train inched along, inviting bushwhackers to attack. None came. Then Charley and a detail of nine other men were assigned to take a train from Cowan on a steep mountain branch line to a village called Tracy City to guard a coal mine.

Tracy City was very poor, made up these days mostly of women and children. The men were fighting on one side of the war or the other. Charley's detail set up quarters in a log cabin, and a widow offered to cook their meals with the rations they brought.

"She was so economical that she could support us ten men and herself and four children with our rations," he wrote home. "And she was a splendid cook and a fine person."

Still, the days and nights were tense. The mountains were full of Rebel raiders. Company E was separated by twenty-one miles from their regiment, which triggered Charley's memories of isolation at Cedar Mountain. This time, though, Union cavalry units nearby were on the alert for surprise raids.

In mid-December they were recalled to Cowan, where they were promised thirty-days' furlough plus bounties from the federal and state governments if they re-enlisted. Charley and most of the rest of the company signed on for another three years.

He told Will, "You know, I may as well take the offer. I have a year left on my enlistment. This commitment is for the duration of the war, and God willing, we'll get those bounties and get out in a year anyway.

"It would be good to be part of a victory, instead of going home and wondering how you and the other boys are doing. Not so sure the folks at home will agree, though."

"Well, we'll be waiting for you after your furlough, and only too happy to tell you what you missed," Will said.

Soon the re-enlisters, now Connecticut Veteran Volunteers, headed home to break the news to their families.

13
Furlough

Charley's papers listed him as "Veteran," meaning he was an experienced soldier who re-enlisted for the duration of the war. Now the hardest part was coming up.

He dreaded telling his father. He could hear the conversation now, even though he felt Gettysburg was the turning point. He was convinced the Union would win. No more talk of compromise or suing for peace. Maybe this war could go on for more than a year, but Charley felt in his bones that there was no turning back.

The three hundred and fifteen Connecticut men made their way home riding on the tops of cattle cars filled with condemned horses to Nashville,

Tenn., and then on to Louisville, Ky. They crossed the Ohio River by boat into Indiana, then by train to New York City on Sunday, Jan. 24.

They slept, unwashed, in the barracks at the New York City Hall, much as they had in the field, to wait until morning for a Connecticut train. Then it was on to New Haven and Hartford. Achy and unshaven, they were honored at a state dinner by proud state officials who didn't seem to mind the state of their hygiene. The next day they turned in their arms for storage until their furloughs were over.

At the South Norwalk station Charley said goodbye to the boys heading to other stations and towns beyond. He and a couple dozen soldiers walked home, taking in the icy peacefulness of the familiar waterfront before turning up Flax Hill or one of the other main roads. The walk was more like a stroll, free from skirmishers and a far cry from a march up hills a lot higher.

His eyes were everywhere.

The oyster boats on the river. The bustle around The Lock Company, the hat company, the corset factory. The shops, the workers' modest houses and the mansions.

Home.

Passersby spotted the deep suntans and beards and wrinkled, torn and grimy uniforms, and approached.

"Charley? John? Ben?"

They were soon surrounded by workmen and shop owners, shaking hands. Young boys joined them, eyes wide-eyed and shining. Charley and his companions couldn't stop grinning, but kept walking.

Charley heard his name called. Jason Black, a gangly black teenager he remembered from oystering, hurried up and held out his hand.

"Mr. Charley, good to see you. Won't be long before I'll be in uniform with you."

"Congratulations. The Navy has had colored sailors since this war began," Charley said.

"No, no. I'm off for New Haven in a couple of days with the Twenty-Ninth Colored Infantry Regiment. Ever since President Lincoln's proclamation, me and my friends have been rarin' to go to free our brothers in the South."

"Infantry. I didn't know."

"Well, you know, no colored fighters in white regiments. We thought we'd go to Massachusetts to sign up with the Fifty-Fourth, the colored regiment formed right after Mr. Lincoln's order, but I wasn't old enough anyway."

He grinned. "Lucky for me the Twenty-Ninth was formed, and I signed up this week. I expect we'll have a commanding officer soon and we'll be off."

"Jason, that's really good news. We need all the good men we can get."

They shook hands again, and Jason turned off at his street. Charley thought about how he enlisted to save the Union. Jason was saving his brothers.

Blacks in the fighting ranks. How would the Rebels deal with them? How would the freed slaves react? In fact, how would the white Union soldiers react? Men in his own regiment joined to keep the Union safe but, like him, many never connected the war with slavery until the President came out with the Emancipation Proclamation.

He put those thoughts on hold as he approached home, the family's white house trimmed in green. Instead of walking right in this time, he knocked on the door.

"Coming!" His mother's voice.

This was Tuesday, and she would be in the kitchen. He smiled, remembering. The irons would be heating on the woodburning stove, with the ironing board and a basket of clean shirts and overalls and dresses nearby.

She opened the door. Her face was flushed from the heat of the work. She looked at him blankly, then flew to him.

"Charley! Charley! Dear Lord! *The Gazette* said some boys would be on furlough. Still, you always come by surprise."

She looked him over quickly. "You're not sick again," she asked anxiously.

"No, Ma," he said grinning. "Just plenty dirty and home for a visit."

She pulled him into the warm house. He dropped his knapsack to hug her. She seemed smaller, rounder. The ironing was forgotten, and they sat at the table as she held both his hands in hers and asking him about his health and the places he had seen. She put out bread and butter.

"Hope this will hold you over till supper," she said. "We'll have whatever catch your father brings home."

"This is just fine, Ma," he said. "Hardtack don't come close to your home baked bread." She laughed when he sniffed the heavy slice he had cut and buttered it thickly. He felt her eyes on him while he ate.

"You eat like our Charley, but you surely have changed," she said, her eyes misting.

"Like how?"

"We'll wait until your brothers and sister and your father come home before I decide altogether.

But first, maybe you want to wash up? Get a pail of water, and I'll heat some on the stove."

He washed and shaved quickly, and wiped down his uniform and shoes as best he could. He wondered how things were going with his friends who maybe went home to the same greeting. His thoughts were interrupted by the sound of excited young voices.

Back in the kitchen, his sister, Hattie, and Henry, Willie, Moses and George, all bigger and different from his sick visit two years ago, were lined up. Hattie spoke up first, rushing over to hug him.

"Charley Hallock, when did you decide to grow a mustache?" she said mockingly.

"It's only a small one," he smiled, smoothing his upper lip with his fingers.

He looked up and saw his father, burly and appraising, just a few steps behind.

"Sir," he said, reaching to shake his hand.

His father pulled him into a gruff embrace. "Glad you're home. Let me wash up and I'll join everyone."

Rubbing his mustache again, Charley turned back to Hattie and his brothers. Hattie talked first, as usual.

"You should see John Knapp. He has so much hair on his face, he looks like he's in disguise. And

Henry. And John Batterson, who came home last summer."

"John was with the Seventeenth Volunteers and wounded at Gettysburg," Charley said. "They fought at Cemetery Hill, not far from us. Fought bravely, even though they lost Lt. Col. Douglas Fowler, that first day. Never found his body."

Hattie grew quiet.

Willie spoke up. "You have your musket?"

"Safe in storage in Hartford."

Charley did a quick calculation. Henry must be sixteen, Hattie, fourteen, Moses, nine, and George, seven. "How old are you now, Willie? Twelve?"

"Yup. Working at The Lock Company. A filer."

"That's how I started. Like it?"

"Better'n school."

Charley nodded. "Keep reading anyway. Everyone in the army seems to have a book or two and we swap them and read anytime we can."

Dad came back into the kitchen and sat down heavily, still smelling of the harbor.

"I hear you've re-enlisted."

Word got around fast.

"I, uh, yes."

"Figured you would. The talk has spread all around town that the twenty or so who got off at South Norwalk today are going back together in a month. When did you plan to tell us?"

Charley flushed. His father was always blunt, but Charley decided he could avoid an argument.

"I felt we should get to greet each other this first day. There's plenty of time to say goodbye later." He kept his eyes on his father's face.

"I need to stay to the end," he added. "We're finally winning some."

The older man grunted. Charley couldn't read his eyes.

"Must be in the Hallock blood," he said gruffly.

Charley eased back in his chair. He had learned since he enlisted that there were plenty of Hallock cousins, some pretty distant, in this war. Even Gen. Halleck was of the clan. There also were some on the Southern side.

His mother and Hattie set the table and placed bowls of steamed clams and boiled potatoes in front of them. Apple pie sat on the sideboard. Charley ate slowly, savoring this first home-cooked meal since his illness in 1861.

"There's a party tonight over at the Methodist Church hall for the soldiers," Hattie said as she passed more bread. "We hear that other volunteers and men discharged with injuries will be there."

Charley's eyes lit up. "I've been thinking a lot about friends who served but weren't in our regiment. It will be good to catch up."

"Some of them also re-enlisted," Henry said.

"Good news," Charley said. "The volunteers are way better than most of the draftees or substitutes for drafted men who paid them to serve in their place. Most are a rough bunch. They're in it for the bonuses. A lot wait until their first payday and then run off to another state to sign up."

"That draft caused some uproar," his father said. "Look at the riots in New York City. It got so bad some coloreds were lynched because draftees blamed them for the war. Slavery and the Emancipation Proclamation and all that. They sure don't agree with Lincoln that slaves should be free."

Charley said nothing. He knew some New York volunteers who fought at Gettysburg and then were shipped home to bring the rioters under control. It was not easy fighting on both sides of the battle. And he thought of Jason Black.

This war sure was complicated.

They ate quickly and got ready for the party. Ma covered a plate of her macaroons with a starched white towel. Charley carried the box of socks and gloves she had knitted during the week.

"We're all in this, you know. The women and girls knit and sew and bring them to the church to be packed and sent to the army. Need some gloves, dear? Pick your own."

Charley stuffed a pair into his pocket. "Thanks, Ma. I'll think of you when I wear them."

"You should see all the factory work for the war effort," Moses said. "Everybody's doing something. The Lock Company is making military hardware, and the workers bought that gigantic flag flying out front of the factory. Other companies have military contracts, too."

They walked down the hill to the big stone church. The bright lights and sounds of the fiddles and a spinet and conversations burst on them as they opened the doors. Charley looked over the scene, taking in a nearly-lost memory of faces. Family and neighbors surrounded him and volunteers from other regiments. Other boys entered, some on crutches or with an arm missing.

Gradually the generations separated, parents in one area, and the school-age relatives and friends in another. Likewise, former and present soldiers shook hands and gave a silent toast.

Sam proposed, "To the misguided among us, and that means all of us, who very shortly will give up the warmth of this hall, the love of family, the home-cooked food, the warm beds, to return to misery and hunger and double-time marches over mountains while being chased, cussed and shot at."

They raised their mugs of cider and drank. Charley looked mockingly into his mug. "What's this? No whiskey?"

"Not here," another sighed dramatically.

A few new soldier-neighbors, some with mends in their uniforms that were hastily stitched before the gathering, introduced themselves.

"Private, Seventeenth Regiment," said John Batterson, dark-haired, with his arm in a sling. "William Smedley here is one of us."

"Nice to meet you," Smedley said in a vaguely British accent. He turned to the pretty blonde girl who had walked up to his side. "This is my sister, Annie."

"Annie." Charley made a small bow. "Pleased to meet an ally, I hope, from across the sea."

"I'm as American as you are. Well, I was born in Manchester, England, but we all became citizens years ago."

Those in uniform talked of the boys they had served with. Most were still in their teens. They talked about incidents where they had to learn to make quick decisions and to follow orders in horrendous battles, sometimes under officers still green under fire who had just graduated from military school or were promoted on the field.

Annie listened attentively, sometimes asking questions. Charley was charmed by her accent, and he turned to talk with her separately, just to listen to her speak and laugh and watch her blue eyes sparkle.

The boys talked lightly of other soldiers who had emigrated from Britain and Germany and Ireland, who fought in their units and mocked each other's accents.

Gradually the background music turned to familiar songs, and the adults and children began singing easily, just as the soldiers did around the campfire or while marching. Listening, Charley was happy to be home. He wished his comrades still on duty could share this one night with him.

The soldiers packed their days with visits with families and friends. They attended many weddings of the Volunteer Veterans, probably more, Charley joked, than the Nutmeg State had ever seen in such a short time. Charley saw Annie nearly every day. They went to parties, on sleigh rides, even to church, to please her.

February sped by, and he asked Annie to write. She smiled. "Every week, if you do."

"Write, even if I can't. It will mean a lot. Letters from home are better than food."

It was a sober day when they boarded the train to Hartford to collect their weapons before going back to Tennessee. Soldiers returning to duty boarded at every stop. They were a solemn bunch.

But not for long. They found humor in everything, even the bumpy ride to the front. Charley described the trip in a letter home:

"We left Connecticut respectably enough, in second class," he wrote. "At Indianapolis, we were transferred to freight cars. We were now Government freight. Plenty of bouncing and bruising.

"Then, of course, we regularly jumped from the cars to push the train up hills, the locomotive having been built by Government contract.

"As one of our own from Company A said so well in the *Connecticut War Record*, if we had our wish, every greenback the contractor received would be turned into a blister, and applied as to render a sitting posture very uncomfortable to that genius for months to come."

14
Bridges

Confederate skirmishers destroyed lines between Desherd and Cowan before the Union troops gained uncertain control in late March.

Charley's regiment was split into ten-man details to guard the railroad and its bridges and tunnels. His detail drew a lonely, gloomy watch at a rail bridge inside the middle of the mountain, where it was always dark and smelled of the damp earth. The men were on edge because the enemy here were civilian Rebel sympathizers who used every chance to tear up the rails.

Luckily, this duty lasted only a month. They were on the march again in late April, struggling over the steep, rough Cumberland Plateau. And then it got rougher.

At Whiteside, Tennessee, they halted on the downside of a steep slope. Before them was a wooden railroad bridge about one hundred feet above a narrow ribbon of water.

"No train to take you across to that mountain," the colonel said, pointing. "You'll do it on foot."

Charley and Will eyed the crossing.

"Must be five hundred, six hundred feet long," Charley speculated.

They could see down through the rails and support structure.

"Can't be a stream," Will said. "Look at the old mill next to it."

"Narrow river, running fast," Charley said. A gusting breeze blew across the gap.

"Come on boys," the colonel urged. "Our own engineers built this one last year, to replace the bridge destroyed by Rebels. If it can hold hundred-car freight trains, it can hold a few thousand of you."

The men continued surveying the bridge, looking down, across, to the other side.

No handrails for support.

Those in front began cautiously stepping, tie to tie. Some behind them started up a chatter. Two or three at first.

"How hard could it be? Hell, we have better odds than when ole Johnny Reb is shooting at us, dead on."

"We make this, and we can face anything."

"Let's do this for dear old Mother."

Charley laughed in spite of himself.

He eyed the men in front inching their way, like they were on a tight rope. Charley stood back, wanting to find the courage to move on.

Some went down on hands and knees. He could do that. He shifted his gear to his back and got down, crawling and gripping the rails. He focused on the back of the soldier ahead and on ties just ahead of his hands. No looking down.

Someone ahead started singing, in a tight voice a little better than a whisper.

"John Brown's body lies a mould'ring in the grave,

John Brown's body lies a mould'ring in the grave,

John Brown's body lies a mould'ring in the grave,

His soul is marching on!"

Charley grimly moved one hand, then one knee, at a time.

"Glory! Glory Hallelujah!

Glory! Glory Hallelujah!

Glory! Glory Hallelujah!

His soul is marching on."

With each "glory," more men joined in. Voices grew raucous.

"He's gone to be a soldier in the army of the Lord!

He's gone to be a soldier in the army of the Lord!

He's gone to be a soldier in the army of the Lord!

His soul is marching on!"

Charley reached the halfway point. He heard himself humming between grunts. They got to the third verse. His eyes were glued ahead but now he was singing, thinking his soul could be one of those if he slipped.

"John Brown's knapsack is strapped upon his back,

John Brown's knapsack is strapped upon his back,

John Brown's knapsack is strapped upon his back,

His soul is marching on!"

By the time they got through the hallelujahs, he had touched land. Terra firma. He staggered off to the side and sank down among the clusters of soldiers waiting for the others. He gulped from his canteen and looked back to the other side, glad that was over.

The boys still on the bridge started on a rowdy version of another marching hymn, *We Are Coming Father Abra'am, Three Hundred Thousand More.* The soldiers around Charley, laughing and cheering, loudly joined in.

"Congratulations," an officer called out as the men continued to arrive.

"You are now in Stevenson, Ala. Keep moving. Another nine miles along the banks of the Tennessee River, and we'll camp for the night at Bridgeport."

His legs still shaky, Charley got up. Will reached him. "Think this is an omen of what's ahead?" Will said, grinning, though he looked as pale as Charley felt.

Charley adjusted his gear. "Almost makes me wish I was back in the Shenandoah Valley with old Stonewall."

Not long after, Lt. Gen. Grant became General in Chief of the U.S. Armies and Gen. William Tecumseh Sherman stepped into Grant's old position as commander of the Military Division of the Mississippi. He also was named commander of the Army of the Cumberland.

In camp, the men learned that Gen. Sherman, their new commander, decided to merge the Eleventh Corps with the Twelfth. They would be the Twentieth, under Gen. Hooker again.

Charley was bummed.

"Our Corps doesn't exist anymore? For two years we marched together, fought together, camped together, ate together. The history of the Twelfth at Cedar Mountain, Chancellorsville and Gettysburg binds us. Hell, the Twelfth was our family."

Will tried to cheer him up.

"Look on the bright side," he said.

"The Twentieth will have our red star. It's now the badge for the old Eleventh, too, though some of those boys say they'll defy the order. Still, the star's the official badge."

"Don't know much about this Sherman," Charley said.

They sought out Henry Davis. The sutler gave them a summary of what he knew.

"West Point graduate. Before the war, he was the superintendent in a Louisiana military college and resigned to take a Union commission. Served at First Bull Run, Shiloh and Vicksburg. The Union lost the first one, won the other two. Word is, he handled himself well as a colonel at Bull Run."

Charley scanned the paper. "Bloody business, all three."

Back in South Norwalk, the news about Sherman caused a little excitement.

"The general has Norwalk roots," his mother wrote.

"His grandfather, Taylor Sherman, was a judge and lawyer here. When the British burned down Norwalk in 1779, he represented the Connecticut Land Company that owned land in Ohio. You may remember your grandfather saying it was part of the Western Reserve once owned by our state.

"After the Revolution, Norwalkers who lost everything in the British attack were allowed to relocate to the Reserve in a section that got to be called The Fire Lands.

"Then Judge Sherman's son, Charles, also a lawyer here, went out to Ohio to look at the land. This was about 1810, after he married Mary Elizabeth Hoyt of our town. He came back to Norwalk to take Mary Elizabeth and his baby son, Charles Taylor Sherman, to Lancaster, on horseback, if you can imagine that.

"They eventually had a large family, as I remember my grandmother saying, and the general was born to Charles and Mary Elizabeth in Ohio in February 1820."

Charley reread the letter. He wondered if he would ever meet the general. Not likely.

"Take care of yourself, Charley," his mother closed. "I saw Annie this morning at the store. She's such a cheery girl."

Charley folded the letter carefully into his haversack.

Their march took them northeast, back into Tennessee, but luckily not over that rail bridge, to the place where many of the men had fought and won the Battle of Lookout Mountain in November 1863.

"We climbed up that mountain. The view was beautiful and grand," Charley wrote to Annie. "Just below we could see the winding Tennessee and Chattanooga Rivers, not three miles away. Looking out across the plateau we could see five states. All one country, no matter what the CSA says."

They moved on, through old battlefields. War sights replaced Nature's glory. They passed the scene of the bloody battle of Chickamauga, where losses were second only to those at Gettysburg.

Boys of the Eleventh Corps and some of the Twelfth had been engaged in the losing slaughter at Chickamauga eight months earlier. Charley and Will marched somberly through a roiled and rough section of the woods and undergrowth where more than 16,000 Union soldiers—including many friends—and 18,400 Confederates were casualties.

The new Twentieth met up with the rest of the army under heavy combat. In the middle of the night they marched on the double for two miles, then laid in the woods, muskets at the ready, all night. The heavily-engaged Third Brigade finally turned the Confederates back.

On the road again.

Wounded men were coming their way from the front, under Rebel artillery fire. Right off, two men from Company I were killed. Another was blinded. The infantry charged and was driven back. Again the Corps spent the night on the ground, watching the shadows.

And so it went. Gen. Joseph Johnston, with fewer than 50,000 Confederate troops and artillery, fought relentlessly, blocking every advance.

Inching closer to Resaca, Georgia, the Union forces were hit by Confederate artillery firing from the hills and by defenders inside the city. The toll was high. Some of Charley's closest friends fired their last shots. Augustus Hoyt, who enlisted with Charley, was among them. He had only two months to go before his enlistment was over.

In Company E, Charley's wounded comrades included Iriah Titus and Samuel Hoyt, Augustus' cousin, and George Bucklee and Henry Barnes of

Fair Haven. Barnes wasn't a Norwalk boy, but still a good and brave friend.

Gen. Johnston retreated south in the middle of the night on May 15 after destroying communications and rail facilities and burning the rail bridges. The battle was a tactical win for the southern leader, and the Union army expected he would hassle them again soon to delay Gen. Sherman's advance. But the Union army wasted no time. The troops arrived in Resaca on May 16 and set out the next day for Atlanta, some 65 miles away.

The weather grew warmer and the men, weary, hungry and dirty, skirmished every day with the Rebel rear guard through a wild, mountainous and uninhabited area.

Hiding behind trees, loading and firing non-stop, Charley could see only a few feet ahead in the brush and gun smoke. He kept up his fire in the direction the bullets came from. In the yelling and shooting, he heard a choked scream next to him. John Robinson, firing into the wilderness from the other side of the same tree, was struck down by a bullet through the cheek.

Charley turned his rifle to where that fatal shot came from, hoping to hit an enemy he couldn't see. Later he thought about the matter of inches that saved him from that bullet. Why was he saved, and not John?

The firing and skirmishing continued, through heat and rain, for nearly two weeks. The stronger the Union army pushed ahead, the more stubbornly the Rebels dug in their heels. The artillery spotted a group of Confederate officers on Pine Mountain and cheered when they brought one down.

The army ground on, gaining headway, through June. Charley's regiment, skirmishers with no breastworks to protect them, filled a gap in the line near Marietta and fought for four hours, driving Rebels back and capturing prisoners. Company E lost four men. Eleven were wounded, including Calvin Hubbard, whose hand was badly burned when his musket burst.

In the heat of this battle the company ran out of ammunition. The men trained their empty guns on the enemy anyway, hoping the Rebels wouldn't realize what happened. Finally a wagonload of ammo arrived and grabbed as quickly as if it had been hardtack to fill their hungry stomachs.

The assault went on for days. The army advanced toward Rebel breastworks at Kennesaw Mountain. The results were brutal, and Gen. Sherman lost 3,000 men in a matter of minutes. Charley began to get that queasy feeling he had at Chancellorsville. But the general quickly changed his tactics to attack from the flank instead of head-on, and the slaughter abated.

Two weeks later, the Twentieth reached the north side of the Chattahoochee River, close enough to see and hear Rebels chattering to each other. Pickets patrolled on both sides. No firing if the other side didn't fire. They openly stared at each other, menacing and increasingly curious.

One day, on Charley's watch, a Rebel guard called out, "Hey, Yank, that coffee sure smells good."

Charley called back, "It tastes even better."

Taunting, he added, "Want some?"

"You bet," the Rebel called back. Other Rebels popped up beside him.

"What will you give me for it?" Charley said, watchful.

The men in Charley's regiment perked up their ears.

"Charley," Will croaked, "What are you doing?"

Charley kept his eyes across the river, his musket ready.

"Well, we have some pretty good tobacco here. Interested?"

"Tobacco," Charley said to Will.

"How do I know you won't shoot me when I get over there?" Charley called.

The Rebel guard put down his gun. "Won't shoot you," he said.

The regiment hashed over the pros and cons.

"Hell," said Murray Jones of Company G, "I'd die for a good smoke. If you go, Charley, I'll go with you."

Charley handed his weapon to Will and stripped down. So did Murray, who by now had collected whatever coffee beans the men had in their tents. They wrapped the beans in towels and lifted them to their heads. They waded into the water.

Charley called back to Will. "They turn unfriendly, take good aim."

Charley pushed across the river with Murray following, careful to keep the coffee dry. The Rebels took the towels and sniffed the beans. They broke into grins and handed over the tobacco. Almost like they weren't the enemy.

"Where're you boys from?" Charley asked.

"These two companies are Jasper Greys, from Savannah," the Rebel picket said. "Part of the First Georgia Regiment. How about you?"

Charley had just named his Connecticut regiment when a burly, red-faced captain swooped down on them.

"What do you think you're doing," he bellowed. "Spying? Consider yourselves captured."

The Rebel picket stepped in front of them.

"Begging your pardon, captain, but these men ain't spying. We called over to them and asked if they had any coffee and they brought it in exchange for tobacco." He held up the towels filled with beans.

"He's right, sir," another piped up. "We asked them to come over."

The captain stood, speechless, glaring from his men to Charley and Murray. When he recovered, he cursed them in a tense, strangled voice, "Get back on your side of the river right quick or I'll send you to Atlanta sooner than you were hoping to go."

Charley and Murray didn't need to be told twice. Still, they managed to wrap up the tobacco first. Back on the north side and with much quiet laughter, they put on their uniforms and split the tobacco with the others.

Will, amused, kept staring at Charley. He shook his head.

"What made you do it? You, of all people?"

Charley didn't answer right away. He had surprised himself, after all his constant talk against men who wanted to break up the Union.

"Dunno," he said finally. "Seemed like a good idea at the time."

A few days later, near sunset, Charley heard a familiar voice.

"Hey, Yank, that coffee sure was good, but it's all gone. We've got some more tobacco. Want another trade?"

Laughing, Charley and Murray made another delivery.

All went well until the same captain spotted them and came running. They hit the water in a hurry before they could collect their reward.

Will met Charley on the shore when he returned, dripping and empty-handed.

"That captain," Charley grinned as he dried off. "Sure is a stiff-neck.

"But I tell you, Will, those Rebels were not what I thought. No swearing at President Lincoln or anything. They were drafted to fight for Georgia. I didn't get the sense they were out and out Yankee haters."

Sure enough, the next night, some of the Jasper Greys deserted and swam over to their camp. Charley didn't get a chance to talk with them. He heard they were sent to Army headquarters somewhere south of the Ohio River. Word came back that they took an oath of allegiance to the Union and were released.

Charley wondered how many others felt like them. Not for long. Gen. Sherman ordered the forces to head out that morning. They inched towards Atlanta.

The general ordered the Twentieth to the supply base at the railroad bridge over the Chatahoochee River. From there, Charley could see the city's church spires, not five miles away.

July came. The South's Gen. Johnston was replaced by Gen. John Hood. The war had put a heavy mark on him—he lost the use of his left arm after Gettysburg and his right leg was amputated after Chickamauga.

"Hood's got more pluck than brains," Charley snorted. "But I expect some pretty hard battles here on in."

Sharpshooters kept busy, picking off Union attackers. Charley's anger hardened with the death of each comrade. One friend who died had a premonition he would never get home, and another was shot twenty-one times in one leg. The regiment lost twenty-three men on July 20.

If Cedar Mountain, Chancellorsville and Gettysburg were bad, he reflected, that day was the hardest battle the Fifth Connecticut had been engaged in as part of this Western Army.

They lost too many good men, but Lt. Col. Henry W. Daboll was an inspiring leader, stubborn and smart. He checked the enemy with his skirmish line and gave the division time to get ready to receive the attack. The colonel was a captain at Cedar Mountain, in that surprise attack by Stonewall Jackson, and Charley felt the colonel had learned a thing or two since then.

In this position of heavy fire, Charley remembered his three-year anniversary of his enlistment on July 22, 1861. He was still nineteen.

"I could be in this army for another three, the way these stubborn Rebels are fighting," Charley said to Will. He thought about the men who had signed up the same day he did and had not re-enlisted. They were home by now. Charley hoped he would join them soon.

He also thought, as he always did, about others who enlisted with him, and would never see Norwalk again.

The muskets grew quiet, but the picket line was plenty busy. The Fifth Regiment was sent forward, rushed the opposing pickets and captured them all. It was an Alabama regiment. The Fifth then took over the rifle pits but the Rebel cannons were lethal.

After dark, the regiment crept close to the mounted sentry and watched for an attack.

Charley was so close he could hear the Rebel sentry spit.

Meanwhile, the Union artillery fired a gun every five minutes into Atlanta. The regiment counted the shots. Twelve, and their hour was up. Another regiment shifted into their position.

"The longest hour of my life," Charley breathed as they settled in the rear.

He wondered, then, how many more he would have.

15
Atlanta

September 1 arrived. After roll call, the sergeant yelled,

"Hallock, report to the colonel's tent."

Will caught up and walked with Charley to the officers' area.

"What do you think it's about, Charley? Trouble? The swim across the river?"

Charley grunted. Will could be a pain. But Charley was worried. The colonel was an easygoing man, slow to anger, and a favorite with the regiment. It would take a lot to rile him. He smoothed out his uniform and removed his cap when he reached the colonel's tent. Will stood outside. The tent flap was up, and the colonel was sitting at his makeshift desk, papers all around.

"Col. Packer, sir? Pvt. Charles Hallock here. You summoned me?"

The officer looked up and smiled distractedly.

"Come in, Hallock."

OK, the news couldn't be bad.

"Just finishing up a little paperwork before we begin our march.

"Need to take care of a few promotions. Including yours."

The colonel stood up and handed him a letter. "Congratulations, corporal."

The colonel's eyes twinkled.

"You're due for a promotion, and you were a big help with the new recruits and those lazy draftees these past four months. Congratulations from me and all the boys of the regiment," and he shook Charley's hand.

He sat down again at the desk and Charley turned to leave.

"And, ah, corporal."

Charley turned back.

"From now on, just don't go sightseeing in places you shouldn't be."

"No, sir."

Will was standing where he had left him.

"Well?"

"Be nice to me, Will. No punishment. I got promoted."

That evening, Charley sat by the fire, sewing the new chevron on his jacket sleeve. Suddenly Atlanta exploded in a blinding light that shook the ground and air. The lookouts reported that the Rebel army blew up rail cars loaded with munitions.

The enemy could be seen withdrawing to the southwest from the city.

Will quipped, "Must be that old Gen. Hood heard you'd been promoted, Charley, and he thought the occasion needed more than a firecracker."

They heard explosions all night and watched huge bonfires licking the nighttime sky.

The next morning, the Twentieth Corps, with the Fifth Connecticut in the lead, marched into Atlanta. They took over school buildings and anything still standing. They found where the explosion had been the night before—only the scorched wheels of eighty rail cars remained on twisted tracks.

Most of the public buildings and factories were destroyed. The damage came from both sides. Rebels did some, to keep anything useful from falling into the hands of the Union army. But Union damage was heavy. Nearly every building had been hit by shells.

Charley was unnerved most by the condition of the Atlantans. Women and children huddled in holes dug in yards as bomb shelters to protect them from the shelling. The roofs were timbers with dirt piled on top.

The retreating Rebel army continued tearing up rails to keep the Union supply trains out. At the same time, scores of hungry Rebel deserters crossed into Union lines from their camp twenty-five miles southwest of the city.

Everything in Atlanta—food to shoes to yard goods for clothing—was scarce and expensive. With supplies stalled outside Atlanta, the Union soldiers foraged locally for food for themselves and their livestock. One day alone, Charley counted 1,000 army wagons hauling ripe corn from a single field planted in the spring by the Rebel soldiers.

Days later, the residents were told they would have to leave the city. It was to be destroyed, brick by brick. The order shocked the Atlantans and the Union soldiers.

Gen. Sherman said he couldn't feed both the army and the people in the war zone, and he offered to provide safe transportation through the military lines to the south, or north by rail to the Ohio River.

Charley and Will read the local newspapers, including articles saying the city officials called the order barbaric. The general wrote in response that it would be barbaric to allow the people to starve.

"This general does have a way with words," Charley said to Will. "Listen."

He read, " 'You cannot qualify war in harsher terms than I will. War is cruelty, and you cannot refine it; and those who brought war into our country deserve all the curses and maledictions a people can pour out. I know I had no hand in making this war, and I know I will make more sacrifices to-day than any of you to secure peace.'

"And here:

" 'But, my dear sirs, when peace does come, you may call on me for any thing. Then will I share with you the last cracker, and watch with you to shield your homes and families against danger from every quarter.

" 'Now you must go, and take with you the old and feeble, feed and nurse them, and build for them, in more quiet places, proper habitations to shield them against the weather until the mad passions of men cool down, and allow the Union and peace once more to settle over your old homes in Atlanta.' "

Charley and the Twentieth Corps remained on watch in the city while Sherman took three other corps and a cavalry division on a chase to prevent Gen. Hood from taking back Atlanta. The Corps sent its sick and wounded soldiers to safety in Chattanooga, repaired the wagon trains, and stocked up on military supplies and cattle for the next move.

Rumors and more than a few lies filled the local papers, describing desperate Union losses. The writers also wrote widely about peace movements up north, where some wanted a quick end to the fighting. In letters, families at home said that was true in Connecticut as well.

His mother wrote that President Lincoln's bid for re-election swirled in debate on the streets of South Norwalk. The arguments focused on the horrifying thousands of casualties, and fueled the ongoing talk about another way out of the war.

The earlier failure of Northern generals to fight decisively, and the death and injury toll of thousands of sons, brothers and husbands who would never come home, or come home with horrific injuries, had never been part of early ambitions of bravery and honor in keeping the country whole.

In bitter arguments, speeches, news columns and editorial cartoons, some supported the struggle to keep the Union intact, and others declared the President had needlessly gotten the nation into a war that could not be won. They called for a settlement without an all-out victory.

Charley wrote back, "Keeping the Union whole is the reason I enlisted. You must vote for the President. I would, if I could. The soldiers who are old enough are backing Good Old Abe and will vote for him. If their states don't allow absentee ballots, the men will go home on leave to vote."

On Election Day, November 8, the federal states endorsed the President in a landslide. Excited and relieved, Charley and Will looked expectantly to the days ahead.

Gen. Grant continued with his strategy to win in Virginia and endorsed Sherman's efforts in Georgia.

On November 14, while floods on the Tennessee River marooned Gen. Hood's army at Florence, Alabama, Sherman and the Union troops that had chased Hood—the Fourteenth, Fifteenth, the Seventeenth, and the cavalry under Gen. Kilpatrick—returned to Atlanta.

The officers relayed the general's orders to the troops, that the army would soon push on to another "somewhere." This time, preparations were a little different. Railroad tracks inside the city were destroyed and telegraph lines were severed. Engineers set fire to every building that could be used by returning Rebels.

Charley wrote to Annie, "A sad sight it was, on this beautiful fall morning, to see so many public and private buildings burning."

He wondered whether the general could ever live up to his peace promise to Atlanta's leaders.

The next day, the Fifteenth and the Seventeenth Corps were organized into a right wing to head southeast toward Macon. The Fourteenth and the Twentieth were to move easterly, toward Augusta. Divided, they would keep the Confederates guessing as to Sherman's true destination.

Four long columns of the 60,000 men in blue marched out of Atlanta that Tuesday. Riding his large bay horse, Sam, the general took turns with one column for a few days, then with another. The men got used to seeing the rumpled general riding with them, often deep in thought. They began calling him "Uncle Billy."

There were times he came out of his reverie to chat casually, and the men were only too happy to talk, or even tell him where they thought the officers could have made better decisions. Smiling, he sometimes allowed they might be right.

One day, riding next to Charley's regiment, he asked where the men were from. When Charley said "South Norwalk, Connecticut," Sherman nodded.

"Nice place, I'm told," he said. "My parents came from Norwalk proper. But Ohio's where I grew up, and in fact there are several very nice cities around the country I would be pleased to call home, once this war's over."

Charley could hardly wait until he had time to send off a note to his family and Annie about the conversation. But as the troops continued tramping along, Charley thought more about their march into the unknown.

"This is eerie, Will," Charley said. "We've been kept in the dark before, but we've never been cut off from headquarters."

"Uncle Billy is fed up with all the rumors. He's out to keep Johnny Reb guessing, and that suits me fine," Will said. "Besides, that keeps the politicians out of our hair."

Charley had to agree. Though he sensed the next few weeks would be unlike what they had lived through so far, his confidence was growing in this general. Sherman focused everything on reuniting the country and limiting bloodshed for his troops, even if it meant the traditional rules of war would have to bend.

Charley reasoned it couldn't be worse than following rules that had them stumbling into disappointment, death, hell, the three long years of this war so far. Other soldiers seemed to sense the same, and they were sober and into their own thoughts at first. Yet it didn't take long before they were joking and singing up and down the long columns.

The first day they marched until they reached a pretty village named Madison. "The country we passed through was very fine," Charley wrote home, even though he couldn't post his letter right away in the embargo. "The nicest we've seen in the state."

Along the way, two men in each company were sent out as foragers under a lieutenant. They brought back cornmeal, bacon, beans, pork and chickens from the farms and towns they passed through. Way better than army provisions. Some days they found plenty, and others, almost nothing for the brigade's commissary wagons. Charley and his fourteen guards were to keep soldiers and the enemy alike from stealing goods in the wagon train.

And they marveled at the freed slaves of every shade, young and old men and women and children, who ran away from the only homes most had ever known, to trail along with the army.

Charley met up with Giles Masen, a young freed slave who had started out helping a member of the One Hundred Twenty-Third New York Regiment before the soldier was sent off on a raid toward Augusta. Charley asked the boy to help the foragers on his team. Giles was smart, likable, filled with stories and quick to help almost before he was asked. This was the first time Charley had a chance to talk at any length with any of the thousands of blacks who followed them.

"You're the way to freedom, Cpl. Charley," Giles said. "The army is our savior."

Charley didn't feel like a savior. These ragged, poor people held so much hope in him and the rest of the boys.

South Norwalk, 1917

"Deacon Taylor," Jesse said, as the sun started sinking below the smokestacks by the railroad, "You were hundreds of miles from the war at that time. You could read only some. You had no radio, no telephone..."

I interrupted him.

"True, there was no radio, no telephone then, but we was paying attention. Most of us couldn't read, like you said, but we knew a lot more than our owners thought we did."

"Like I told you, Marse got his information from the local newspapers, just like the other plantation owners did, unless they had kin in the war. The newspapers didn't always talk about losses. Sometimes it seemed they even made victories up. And sometimes they talked about what the northern papers said. We listened to the owners discuss it all.

"We also knew a lot of slaves just up and fled the plantations, especially after President Lincoln was re-elected and the Union army began the march through Georgia.

"I remember one day when Marse seemed in a worse mood than usual. Even the Missus was beside herself, talking about the stories she heard where the Union army spread itself out sixty miles wide, grabbing up food from the houses and the fields, destroying animals and sometimes taking only part of the carcasses.

"She called them monsters, animals, murderous thieves with no thought of how hard the plantation owners worked to put food on the table.

"I ran and located Louie and Mose. I waved my stick around at the crows and told the boys what I overheard.

" 'All the white folks is pretty nervous those Yanks are coming our way,' Mose said.

" 'Suppose they do get this far and mess up this plantation. Take all the food, take the horses and wagons and such? I hear they's burning plantations." He shook his head.

" 'What will happen to us?' " Louis said.

" 'Marse has that look in his eyes that could murder, all by itself. Whichever way this goes, it ain't gonna be good for us.

" 'Lots ran away to the free states. Some were brought back, and was punished fierce.' "

" 'Worse, the dogs got some of them, ' Mose said. We was silent, just thinking how that was.

"But others got away," I pressed.

" 'Hunh,' " Louis said. " 'We don't know what happened. We don't know they better off now.' "

Jesse listened to me in silence.

"So what did you do?" he asked. "Did you run away?"

I shook my head. "Not then. The Union army was too far away. But I knew Marse and Louis and Mose had to be wrong. Something big was happening.

"I could see for myself, when Missus took me with her into town to carry packages. Old familiar faces was missing. The only answer was, they made it somehow. If they was dead, the masters would have said so, to keep the fear in the rest of us.

"They gone to freedom, those slaves did. They gone to meet the Union. They was winning now."

I stopped and looked at Jesse. "Just talking about those days is getting me excited. It was a powerful time. And Charley, he told me when I told him what was happening on the plantation, that the time held some powerful emotions for the Union soldiers, too. They learned more about the reason for the war on that March to the Sea, that three hundred miles from Atlanta to Savannah, than they learned in the whole rest of the time they was in the Army.

"They learned by what they saw, and they learned from the 11,000 men, women and children who left their owners to join the Union march."

I felt my eyes burning with fire, and I could see Jesse was listening in awe. I stood up and stretched.

"I see your mama poppin' her head out the door, Jesse. Your supper must be ready. The next time I see you, jes' listen, and I'll try to explain how it all happened, like I remember Charley Hallock did."

I sat for a while longer and thought about that amazing time, and Charley's words.

16
To the Sea

Sherman's army continued its secretive, divided drive eastward.

Charley searched for local newspapers whenever the Twentieth passed through towns. Plenty was written about Gen. Grant, commander of all five Union armies, looking to Richmond with 120,000 troops, to take on Gen. Lee. But the newspapers, spies, politicians and other officials knew next to nothing about Sherman and his 60,000 men somewhere in Georgia.

Since the teletype lines had been cut and mail and new supplies could not be delivered, spies and reporters could only find out only where Sherman had been. They speculated a lot about where he was going.

Meanwhile, Union foragers scoured the countryside daily, invading plantations and rich and poor farms, filling wagons with cornmeal, meat and sweet potatoes. Some days were bountiful, some lean. Still, Charley and his companions ate a lot better than they did in the days of Cedar Mountain, Chancellorsville and Gettysburg and the long marches leading up to Atlanta.

Pretty quickly, the isolation from Washington headquarters and the conditions on the march took an interesting turn. The men were confident they could do almost anything the general asked, and he didn't insist on small details, like requiring that uniforms and gear be in top condition, or that the soldiers follow strict military order.

Charley sometimes thought about the uniform he was so proud to put on when he enlisted, and the silver watch and handmade shoes he bought for himself at home. Now, his face was unshaven, his hair was shaggy, his watch and shoes long gone. Jokes passed through the ranks about the last time anyone bathed.

The clothes on their backs were torn. Parts of pant legs or sleeves were missing. They hacked off pieces of their frock coats to patch embarrassing tears in their pants. Many swapped their sorry-looking rags for castoffs of the fleeing Confederates, as a kind of trophy of war.

Sometimes the "uniform" was pants and a shirt that had been hanging on a farmer's clothesline.

Not that the Southern boys had much. Charley could see, by the bodies of dead Rebel soldiers, that more than a few had taken to wearing Union castoffs themselves.

Very hungry Rebels. Charley was struck by how emaciated their bodies were.

"Starving, Will, worse than our boys."

The answer had to be that they, like he, were fighting on more than food.

Charley and his brigade's commissary guards kept an eye on the wagons and mules, but also helped clear roads, chop down trees and lay corduroy roadways through the swampy areas. Sometimes the corduroy got to be three layers thick when tree trunks sank into the wet sandy ground under the weight of the wagons and artillery.

If they complained about the bugs, the thorny bushes or even the poison ivy, they also grew more confident. They had overcome so much. The closer the general led them to their goal, the sooner they were to going home, and the angrier, even more vengeful, they got. The Confederates should pay for this awful war.

Watching the blacks who trailed them patiently was an eye opener for Charley. They carried their possessions in cloth bundles in their arms or on their heads or in carts or carriages. They wore rags. Many continued to build roads while the soldiers slept. Yet they seemed tireless and joyful.

Those who couldn't join the march gathered along the roadside as the army passed, just to catch sight of Gen. Sherman. Charley wondered how they knew his name or recognized him, when they couldn't read and there was no advance news about where the troops were heading.

Sitting around the fire evenings, sometimes watching blacks entertain with wrestling matches and gospel songs, Charley and Will traded stories with Giles about the ways of the South and the North.

Charley knew a handful of blacks in Norwalk. They were free for as long as he had known them. Henry Davis said there were three and a half million slaves in the South. Charley couldn't get his head around the huge number.

He caught sight of the hardships Giles described when he least expected it. Like the time Giles was washing his shirt in the river. His bent back was laced with raised scars.

"Sometimes the master got carried away and just kept whipping," Giles explained, shrugging. "Them's the times I knew I had to find a way to leave, or I would die."

The talk around the fire also created smiles.

Some blacks joked about what they expected when the federal soldiers arrived.

"Our masters told us that the Yankees was different from the white men we knew," Giles said. "They put plenty of fear in our hearts by telling us you was the devil."

Charley remembered the Virginia newspapers that Northerners had horns on their heads.

"I don't know what else they told you, but I'll be honest. In this army, you'll find more than a few who will not be friendly. They volunteered to keep the country whole. They don't necessarily see the connection between secession and slavery."

Giles nodded soberly. "We already know that. Some have cursed us, and worse. Still, we'll take our chances and do what we can to help you win so we can be free. We—I—don't want to be owned by anyone."

The Corps shifted southeast and entered a little town called Eatontown. There, Lewis Beecher of Charley's company foraged a little too far from the line of march and was captured by the Rebel calvary. Rumor had it that he was taken to Andersonville Prison, an open, overcrowded stockade notorious for filthy conditions and lack of food.

Charley's anger about the stories of prison conditions deepened as they tramped through lush areas of the Georgian countryside. "There's plenty of food in the state," he said to Will. "There's no excuse for the starving and neglect of thousands of our boys."

By November 23 they reached Milledgeville, a small country town that was the state capitol. They continued east, destroying rail lines along the way.

The land turned sandy, shifty. Foraging grew harder.

Three days later they reached Sandersville. Rebel cavalry and the local home guard militia showed themselves every day. Still the Yank forces moved relentlessly east.

"Looks as though we'll eventually bring up at Savannah," Charley said to Will. "You were right. You win the bet. Best I can do is pay you with this Confederate money." He handed him a faded hand-drawn bill.

"Keep your souvenir," Will said, pushing the bill back at him. "Pay day is coming. I'll take hard Union cash when our ship comes in."

Charley laughed. "You'll be sorry. This could become a rare work of art."

They entered a barren stretch of sand and large pine trees. The brigades took turns in the lead, grateful when they were in the front lines of the march before the corduroyed roads got churned up.

The troops reached Davisboro and methodically destroyed the Georgia Central Railroad. On November 27 alone, they tore up more than forty miles of track. They burned the tracks and bent the heated iron rails around trees, into a twisted shape they nicknamed "Sherman's neckties."

Rebels retreating before them burned newly harvested cotton to keep it out of the hands of the invaders, and Sherman's soldiers torched even more.

All the while, Nature seemed to be throwing every obstacle at them as well—freezing weather, wet, thorny briars, poisonous undergrowth, fleas, snakes, even alligator scares. The closer they got to Savannah, the swampier the terrain grew.

But they knew now that Savannah was the destination. A port on the Atlantic. As far as they could go before they turned north, toward home.

They arrived near the city on December 12. Gen. Sherman and his officers headed to the shore to wait for the Union naval fleet to arrive with supplies of guns, ammunition, food, clothing, and especially, shoes. Soldiers let out a cheer when they spotted several large schooners flying the federal colors, and a large steamboat riding anchor. They signaled the fleet with flags. The ships in turn signaled that they were ready to give support to the capture of Fort McAllister, the last Rebel fort between the army and Savannah.

Not that their help was needed. Brig. Gen. William Hazen's Division of the Fifteenth Corps quickly overpowered the fort's Confederate defenders.

The regiment was detached from the brigade and sent with empty supply wagons to the Ogeechee River, by the fort, to wait for the fleet. The river fed into the Ossabaw Sound and its beautiful white sand beaches, which in turn fed into the Atlantic Ocean. Charley breathed in brisk salt air for the first time since leaving South Norwalk.

The engineers set about building a wharf so the ships could unload cargo. The first steamboat making its way up the Ogeechee was *The Island City*.

"Will," Charley exclaimed. "Unless that's a copy, that boat once ran between New York and Norwalk."

"You sure?" Will strained to see. "Wait, I think you're right. What a sight."

This familiar boat now carried a precious cargo of six weeks' worth of mail for the 60,000 homesick men of the Army of the West. Charley and his men joyfully loaded the precious sacks of letters into the first wagon.

Next, the schooners tied up and off-loaded military supplies and hardtack, port, sugar, coffee and bacon. One wagon after another was filled and moved on.

Charley looked down into the sandy waters edging the Sound and saw a sight that was so much a part of his life back home.

"Oysters!" he cried. "Boys, we are in for a treat tonight."

His detail filled two wagons and set out for Savannah.

The troops continued their struggles through swamps on the north and west sides of the river and were hassled by the city's garrison, but they also managed to take in a large store of rice from mills along the Savannah River.

Along the way, joyful news traveled up the long wagon file from the men ahead: The Rebel troops under Gen. Braxton Bragg had evacuated Savannah by crossing the Savannah River into South Carolina. The city surrendered to Gen. Sherman on December 21, and the army was led by the Twentieth Corps to occupy the city.

The general ordered that the rice be set aside to help feed hungry people of the city.

The day of the surrender was the day the rest of the country finally learned where Sherman and his troops were. He telegraphed President Lincoln, saying he was presenting the city as a Christmas gift to him, along with one hundred and fifty guns and ammunition and 25,000 bales of cotton.

That also was the day Charley learned that a general of the Fourteenth had led hundreds, maybe thousands, of black followers to their deaths earlier in the month.

Word was, the Fourteenth crossed the swollen waters of Ebenezer Creek over pontoon bridges on the way to Savannah. When the last soldier touched land, the general had the bridges quickly removed. The black followers were stranded. Panicking, not wanting to be left to the mercy of Confederate soldiers in pursuit, they tried to cross by swimming, and many drowned.

Charley was thunderstruck. These were our friends, our uncomplaining helpers and guides. Is this how we would deal with them at the end?

Even Washington was alarmed. The Secretary of War met with Sherman and local black leaders to figure out what happened. The black leaders stood by the general and said he had no part in the decision. The general proposed that the federal government give confiscated land to the former slaves to give them a place to live and work in the South, but the plan fell through.

Back in Bear Creek, Marse read the order in the newspaper. I heard him cackle, "That will never happen. The Yanks will never win, no matter what. But those slaves know by now what I've known all along—the North will never let them be free."

17
Heading North

The winter of 1917 came and passed before I saw Jesse again.

We met on a cold March day at Bethel A.M.E. Church, on Knight Street. I was the church's treasurer then, busy raising money for a building we would own instead of rent.

I poked my head in the doorway of the community room, and could feel a grin spreading across my face at the sight of Jesse and his friends from the tutoring class.

"I'm glad to see you boys."

"Really?" Jesse said. "Are we in some kind of trouble?"

" 'Course not, Jesse. I was just thinking about how this month is the anniversary of the time I met the Union soldier who brought me to my home of freedom. That was fifty-two years ago."

Jesse's friend Willy whistled. He looked up at the clock on the wall.

"We have some time before we head home," he said. "Jesse told me, and Amos and Leroy here, some about Cpl. Charley and you back in the Civil War. Can you tell us, too?"

"I'm always happy to tell this story." I eased into a chair by the table and sat quiet for a minute, thinking.

"I'll start with a little more about Charley."

Charley said he liked the stay in Savannah just fine. He liked the way the city looked, with its wide streets, parks and big oaks, trees he hadn't seen since Connecticut. He thought the folks actually were glad they were there.

It helped the soldiers' spirits that they could wash up and begin to feel normal. They had fresh uniforms and shoes and other supplies the ships brought in.

The mail from home made the biggest difference. The sacks of letters were brought south in those U.S. Navy ships, and it didn't take much time for the men to fill them again with letters of their own to their loved ones.

But they knew their journey in this war was not finished.

Charley had no doubts they would go home winners. They had the skills and confidence, after all the marches, in territory they could never have imagined on the long six-week haul from Atlanta to Savannah, to get the job done.

Finally, on January 16, they set out for South Carolina, ready to mostly forage again for their food and supplies as they had in Georgia.

"Uncle Billy's made it plain he'll be hard on South Carolina, seeing as how they started all this trouble," Charley said.

He and Will rested on their rifles with the rest of the First Division on the banks of the Savannah River. It would soon be their turn to cross by pontoon bridge into the Palmetto State.

"They're sure to not like us any better than they did when they took the fort," Will said. He checked the ammo in his haversack and moved his hardtack to reach it better.

It didn't take long to see Mother Nature and the Rebels had teamed up again to challenge the Union army.

The division and the followers crossed the river into South Carolina and got stuck in mud, and lots of it. The causeway through the lowlands was under water, and two bridges had washed away. They struggled some sixty miles north to Sisters Ferry, opposite Savannah, to wait for the Second Division to cross.

On the way they stopped for the night, surrounded by muddy rice fields. The land seemed dry enough for the army to set up camp.

It wasn't dry for long. Rushing, icy water woke them in the middle of the night. Swearing, the men grabbed their soaking tents, gear, weapons and supplies. Clearly, someone unfriendly had raised the water gate to flood the field.

"So this is South Carolina," Charley muttered as he shivered. It was a sorry-looking army that took to the road as dawn broke.

In Lexington, the Union cavalries tangled with Rebel cavalries, and that led to fires through the town.

The army and followers moved on, in hard-blowing weather for another thirteen miles, to just south of Columbia, the state capital. Thousands of Union soldiers of the Fifteenth and Seventeenth Corps had already crossed the Congaree River into the pretty city.

Charley could see thick black smoke over Columbia. "I thought we were planting our colors," Charley said. "Not burning the city down."

He soon heard that Columbia officials accused the Union soldiers of destroying the city. A few days later, they met up with troops from the Thirteenth Iowa, who raised the U.S. flag over the Columbia state house, and they told a different story.

"No question about it, their Gen. Wade Hampton ordered those fires," one Iowan told Charley.

"When we landed, the streets were lined with bales of cotton and the Rebels were setting fire to them. In that wind, the fires were soon out of control, no matter how hard our boys of the Fifteenth and Seventeenth battled to put them out. The fires burned through the night."

But then Charley also heard that some Union soldiers were at fault, too. Even the general allowed that it was possible. Still, Charley felt it was a setup by city fathers against Sherman's army.

Gen. Joseph Johnston, the same southern leader who fought at First Manassas and dogged their every move toward Atlanta in the spring and summer, again fought them at every turn. Rebel troops who had fallen back from Wilmington, North Carolina, also hassled them. They advanced, though it was slow-going in the frigid weather.

Charley and Will were in the troops laying down more corduroy roads of fence rails and small trees.

The men once again looked like the tattered army that crossed Georgia. Again they were barefoot, their clothing torn, their faces covered by tangled beards. Again, military order was stomped out in that mud.

Rumors traveled faster than the troops. Local papers in Winnsboro guessed the army probably was heading to prison camps in Charlotte and Salisbury in North Carolina to free soldiers there. But that didn't happen.

Five weeks after Savannah, Gen. Sherman had the troops turn east instead of north. They pushed through freezing rain and more mud, foraging and skirmishing with the enemy cavalry. They moved from the lowlands and crossed the Catawba River by pontoon bridges. The country grew hilly.

Charley said hopefully that the land was beginning to look like Connecticut.

"Wishful thinking, Charley," Will grumbled. "I swear we'll run out of fences and trees for corduroying. The wagons and artillery will sink out of sight before we get wherever we're going."

Charley groaned. "I know I signed up for the duration, but this hell has got to end soon."

March 12, they crossed another state line, reaching the Great Pee Dee River and North Carolina. At Fayetteville, on the Cape Fear River, the army was met by two steamboats loaded with mail and shoes. Their spirits lifted and their feet covered again, the men got the news the next afternoon that the brigade was ordered to fall in for a review by the general.

Charley laughed.

He rubbed his torn and calloused hands and cuts and bruises, and glanced at his pants ripped short at the knees and patched. His head was covered by a wide-brimmed slouch hat to keep the rain out of his eyes. He couldn't remember the last time he washed or shaved, and lice drove him crazy. Maybe even worse than before Savannah.

He looked around at the army of 60,000, his comrades day and night for three months, mostly cut off from civilized society.

Some led dogs or other animals in the swamps on leashes, or had tamed them enough to sit on their shoulders as they marched. Some pets even rode on the mules in the supply train.

But the men were cheerful, even in their cursing. They talked about keeping their eyes toward Richmond and the traitorous CSA. They trusted Uncle Billy to take them to victory and home. The general smiled as the troops passed in review.

Charley heard him joke to an aide, "My ragamuffins."

They found more enemy at Averasboro, North Carolina. Lt. Col. James L. Selfridge sent Charley's regiment on March 16 to try to dislodge them in a three-hour fight before nightfall. The Fifth Connecticut lost an officer, three men were killed, eleven were wounded and eleven went missing.

The Rebels pulled out before dawn.

Some regiment officers argued that while the official report said this was a skirmish, it was really a full-blown battle. In all, the division captured three cannon, two hundred and seventeen prisoners, sixty-eight wounded. The division buried one hundred eight Rebels and captured and destroyed one hundred forty-three Enfield rifles.

"The weapons were an arsenal that had been used all through the war by the Confederates," he wrote home. "Our men destroyed it so it could do no more harm."

Fighting continued all the way to Goldsboro, North Carolina, a key railroad junction for Southern supply lines. The miles-long army struggled over cold rain-soaked roads so bad that the mules were unhitched and men pulled the wagons through the worst areas.

Swollen creeks were too wide to go around and the men waded through, sometimes in waist-high water. All the while, they were on alert for skirmishers or worse.

On March 23 they reached the city, where the Atlantic and North Carolina Rail Road intersected with the Wilmington and Weldon Rail Road, the longest rail line in the world, and the last line available to Gen. Lee to supply and transport his troops.

18
The Yanks

Savannah to Goldsboro was a four hundred twenty five-mile drive, and still the Union army got there in less than nine weeks. Charley said he saw Goldsboro, population 4,000, like a pretty village.

He poked Will as they closed in on Goldsboro. "Take a look at the bandbox soldiers over there," he said, pointing to the proper military formations of 20,000 men in clean, regulation uniforms just ahead. They were the men led by Gens. John Schofield and Alfred Terry up from Wilmington, who would join them on the final stretch north.

"Hm," Will said. "We'll have to break them in to look like real fighting men."

"Could be these Rebs will do it for us," Charley said.

Goldsboro area farmers and families lined the roads to take in the sight of Sherman's 60,000-man infantry, artillery and cavalry, and the freed men, women and children followed by cattle, horses and mules. Sherman's "ragamuffins" were not much like any army they had seen before.

Truth was, Charley said, the soldiers were only too anxious to set up camp and clean up to feel human again.

Mail arrived, and Charley read every letter from home over and over. South Norwalk seemed closer than ever, yet too far away. He almost felt shy reading Annie's account of events, of raising funds and packing packages for her brother and for him. He smelled her sweet sachet and tucked it into his shirt pocket.

The sutlers came back into camp, and Henry Davis was among them again. His tent and wagon were loaded with supplies and newspapers.

Gen. Sherman went off to Richmond to consult with Gen. Grant about the last leg of the fight.

"He wants to take this army to Richmond, to have the satisfaction of finishing the job he started in Atlanta," Davis predicted. "But there's talk that Grant wants him to settle things first with Johnston."

Charley grunted. "We fooled Johnston enough times about where we were headed since Atlanta. He's stubborn."

The army's rows of white tents rose on the outskirts of the town, with the officers settled toward the rear. Sutler tents rose behind them. The cooks set up their wagons and began the work of feeding the army. Soldiers cleaned up, shaved and put on new uniforms.

Charley assigned guards to the pens holding the mules.

At dark, fires dotted areas between the tents as far as the soldiers could see. The men gathered round, relaxing, playing cards, reading books and newspapers and tending to letters as usual. Some wrestled or played ball.

Lately, they worried less about ambushes.

Since Savannah, more and more soldiers joined the prayer groups off to the side.

During the day, the army was kept busy answering roll calls and repairing wagons for the final leg home. They waited impatiently for supplies of rations and ammunition that they loaded in wagons for wherever they were headed next.

Freed slaves continued to flock to the camp.

The Ebenezer Creek deaths weighed heavily on Charley's mind. He was anxious to get home, but there were loose ends to be tied up before then.

"So there they was, just thirty miles from my plantation," I said to the boys sitting around the church hall table.

"By this time, Marse and the Missus knew they was on the losing side. They didn't plan to stay around for a visit from any foraging Union soldiers. They was going to try to make it to Louisiana, which they figured was safer than South Carolina. And us slaves was on our own.

"I had other thoughts. I was thinking about my freedom all these four years, ever since I heard the men from the North was coming. I wanted to see where being free could take me, what I could do with it. I just had to think about how I could reach those Yankees.

"Turns out the Army came to me. My chance came on March 28, 1865. I'll never forget the date.

"About twenty Union men with wagons came to Bear Creek, spreading over plantations and taking corn from the cribs and the hams curing in the smoke houses. Slaves who had not already run away was helping soldiers load the food in any wagons they could find.

I ran into the meadow and led one of our mules and a wagon back to a bunch of soldiers taking apart the corn crib.

" 'Whoa, little man, what are you bringing us?' a soldier called out.

"You need something to carry that corn?" I watched him, wondering what he would do.

He led the mule and wagon toward the pile.

"I know where there's sweet potatoes," I said. He turned back, and nodded.

I ran over to the house and started digging. I uncovered the dirt storage bin.

"Good, son. Thank you." The soldier called others to help. I followed, and helped load the wagon. When the soldiers was ready to leave, I spoke up.

"Take me with you?" I held my breath. Would they take me? Maybe not. I remembered Ebenezer Creek.

The soldier didn't even seem to think about it. "Sure. Jump in."

My heart was pounding, I can tell you. Then another brother jumped in next to me. He looked older, and he was wearing what the soldiers was wearing.

"Name's Giles," he said.

"Jimmy John. You with the army?"

"Been traveling with the Union soldiers since Atlanta. Helping them forage and talk with the locals—freed slaves that is—to find the best roads and farms, and where there were skirmishers nearby."

"Can I do that? I know the area hereabouts and can work hard."

Giles shrugged. "Maybe. Wait till you get to camp. You'll see how many others want to do the same."

We rode along, him telling me how he worked in the city and ran away from his white family just before Atlantans was ordered to leave. He befriended one officer and worked for him, then worked with two other Yanks from New York and Connecticut.

The closer we got to Goldsboro, the more soldiers and wagons we saw. The wagons was full of food, furniture and ladies clothes and stuff. Not hardly war supplies. One soldier had a top hat on his head. Some Yankees looked a little rough, like.

We reached camp, bigger than any city I ever seen. Supply wagons and horses and mules was on one side. White tents was set up, with roads between groups of them. There was signs posted on sticks. I asked Giles what they said.

"The army is divided. This here is the Fifteenth Army Corps, that's the Seventeenth, over here is the Fourteenth, and that's the Twentieth. The sign with the red star is the first division of the Twentieth, and that's where we'll unload the wagons."

The drover guided them to the supply area near the big stoves. A dozen soldiers waited by the sign post.

"Help hand down the food," Giles said to me. "Then I'll introduce you to the boss of my detail, Cpl. Hallock."

South Norwalk, 1917

"Deacon Taylor, was you scared when you got into camp?" Jesse asked.

"My heart was jumping in my chest like a frog in a contest," I said. "But it was more that I was excited like never before. I wasn't scared exactly, not like when Marse was on a rampage. I was afraid they might not take me along.

"Then I met the corporal."

19
The Corporal

Cpl. Hallock didn't look much like the foragers I came to camp with. He had on a clean uniform with no rips I could see. I guessed his haircut was new, 'cause he had a tan but his neck was bright red. His shoes looked new. He rattled off orders to soldiers guarding the place where the cooks was and the mules that hauled the wagons.

Used to watching white folks, I liked what I saw. This Yankee was soft spoken but had a look in his eyes that said you couldn't mess with him.

"Cpl. Charley," Giles said. "This here's Jimmy John, who helped us find and load food at a plantation in Bear Creek. He wants to join us."

I stood watchful, still as a stone, just a little behind Giles. The corporal turned around to look me, barefoot and wearing a torn shirt and pants that was way too big.

He sighed.

"Jimmy John. Nice to meet you. You about twelve?"

"No suh." I heard my voice boom, I was so nervous. "I'm fifteen or sixteen." The soldiers shook their heads.

Charley's squinted and looked me over again. "Gotta get your story straight. Which is it? Fifteen, or sixteen?"

"Don't rightly know, suh. That's what the Missus said I was. She didn't know for sure."

"Ah. And why do want to come with us?"

"Well, suh, I want to put on my new Cloak of Freedom and go North to start a new life."

"Cloak of Freedom," Charley repeated.

He looked out over the thousands of black men, women and children helping all over the camp. "All these folks are bent on somehow keeping their new freedom," he said. "But once the army stops foraging, there won't be enough food to go around. And what will they do when we leave? There's no way they can all go North."

Ebenezer Creek proved that. But I just watched him.

"Your family with us, too?"

"No, suh. Don't know where any of the family is. They long gone. Sold. So it's just me."

He gave me a long look I couldn't read.

"I don't know about that cloak," he said at last, "but we can do something about your clothes.

"Giles, see if you can find him something decent. And shoes. And a hat. Wash up. Then both of you come back here and I'll have work for you before the midday meal." He turned back to the men of his detail.

Giles and I made our way to the wagons filled with new uniforms. "Delivered in the last couple of days," he said. "Just in time, to replace our rags."

Giles pulled out pants, a shirt, socks and shoes, and a cap, and handed them over to me.

"You might not be able to wear the shoes all the time, seein' as how you don't have any now, but break them in," he said. "When we leave this camp, your feet'll feel a lot better on the march.

"Of course, that's if the corporal says you can go with us."

I changed into the new clothes and fiddled to make the cap fit. I knew what the corporal said about everyone wanting to go with the army, but I felt inside I already had one foot out of North Carolina.

We walked back to Cpl. Charley's detail. "Giles, you going north?"

"I expect so, but not with the army," he said. "I ran away from my owner when the Yanks was in Atlanta. Since then my family's gone to Canada, through the underground railroad, and I aim to find them when this is over. This army's mostly been good to me, and I'll help them until I get close enough to get to my family.

"But tell me, Jimmy John, how old are you, really?"

"Like I said, fifteen or sixteen. I know you're asking because I'm small. I'm the runt in my family. My brothers are bigger. If they's still alive. How old're you?"

"Sixteen in April. You come just to my shoulder, so you know why the corporal has his doubts."

We reached the commissary area, where the mules were hitched, three to a side, to the wagon poles, eating their oats. I gave them a wide berth.

Cpl. Charley was watching.

"I see you know something about these animals."

"Yes suh, they kicks fearsome. I steers clear of their rear. I even steers clear of their fronts."

The drovers laughed.

"Well, our job is to make sure nobody steals them, even in this fine army," Cpl. Charley said. "Sometimes a soldier will lose a mule somehow and take one of ours. It happens more often than you think. When we're on the march or in camp we're always on guard, and sleep under the wagons to make sure. We even eat together."

"And these being the commissary wagons, we sometimes eat pretty good," Giles said on the side.

So much was going on in the gigantic camp. All day long, trains pulled into the depot with supplies from Washington. Locomotives hauled maybe twenty-five cars of clothing, medical supplies and ammunition each.

I tagged after Giles, eager to show I could do anything the corporal or he asked me to do. I filled the animal troughs with corn or oats and water. I hauled potatoes and corn and hams to the cooks. I watched the mountain of food go down to nuthin' that same day. I ate meals I never ate on the plantation.

All the while, the mule drovers cracked their "black snakes" to make the mules pay attention.

The mules liked to act up, fighting and jumping the center pole to attack mules on the other side. When that happened, the drovers let out a string of cuss words the likes I never heard before. I grinned at Giles.

Giles nodded. "Notice how those mules have such big ears? Those drovers have language you ain't heard yet, but it's how to get into those stubborn brains." Sure enough, as we watched, the tangle of pole and bodies and legs that got the drover to swear at them was untangled in a flash. The mules munched on feed like nothing happened.

Some men nearby was chattering in a way I couldn't understand.

"What're they saying, Giles?"

Giles looked over to where I was pointing.

"Them? They're German, Russian, Polish, Swedish, Italian, British, Irish. You name them, we got 'em. Only about half our soldiers were born in this country. And even those are hard to understand sometimes because they use different words and ways to pronounce them. Depends on where they're from, Massachusetts, New York, Wisconsin, any of the states."

I didn't know any white foreigners, and hardly any places Giles mentioned. I tried to figure how all these people were so different and still could be American.

"I know what you mean," Giles said. "Cpl. Charley and I talked about it, and he said being American was maybe the only thing they had in common. They could be different in everything else, except in believing in making the Union whole and getting back home."

I had a lot to think about that night. Not all of it was good. A big part was the shock of seeing up close that Marse might have been right about some of the Northerners.

Cpl. Charley, Giles and me took a walk into town. Everywhere, men in blue was trading horses and mules from farms and plantations. Some had mules pulling fancy town carriages. Some stood on street corners or between buildings, selling watches and jewelry and gold and silver. They was gambling at faro and poker, with money and things they had taken from peoples' homes.

They was even cheating each other.

Cpl. Charley and Giles talked about Uncle Billy Sherman, who brought them to the doorstep of the home of the Confederacy. Mostly, they said, he fooled the Rebels pretty well.

Never had I heard Marse or anyone else on the plantation call the southern military leaders "uncle" or any other type of kin. They was always proper. It was "the general" or the title and the name, like Gen. Lee or Gen. Johnston. They had respect. The northerners showed a different attitude. Like they was more equal, even though they obeyed orders.

Cpl. Charley thought maybe I had a point. "As to generals, we sometimes call them "uncle" when we feel they care about our welfare," he said. "We've had our share where that didn't seem to be. As for obeying orders, that's what soldiers are trained to do. Can't have them do whatever they please on the battlefield. So we can like our generals even as family and obey them at the same time."

About a week later, resting after the evening meal, I took in the soldiers sitting around their fires. Some sang patriotic songs, songs of home and hymns. Some off to the side were reading the Bible together. Some just listened to my brothers and sisters and their gospel singing.

Charley was writing a letter by the light of a candle pressed in the end of a bayonet stuck in the top of the table.

"You go to church, Cpl. Charley?" I asked.

"Sometimes." But he didn't look like he wanted to talk tonight. He kept writing.

"That letter's probably for Annie," Giles said as he stirred the fire. "He's been writing her nearly every night now, so he can make the morning posts."

Cpl. Charley looked up. He shook his head and smiled.

"Already took care of Annie's letter," he said. "This one's to my folks, Jimmy John, and it concerns you."

I could feel my eyes pop wide. "Me?"

Cpl. Charley sighed. "Got a letter today from my father, asking what we were going to do with all the ex-slaves who've been following us since Atlanta. Dad and I, well, we never have quite seen eye-to-eye over any part of this war."

"Cpl. Charley, I'm not following what you're saying?"

"No disrespect to my Dad, Jimmy John, but we've had our differences. When I thought it was only about bringing the South back into the Union, he said we were just off on a lark. Then when the President said it was about Emancipation, he was disgusted. Said slaves in other states were not part of our responsibility."

The corporal put his pencil down and turned to face me.

"I need to make my father understand about folks like you, and how you and all these former slaves had no control over your lives. Yet you all helped us in so many ways. People back home need to understand that this war, bad as it was and still is, had a deeper purpose that will only make our country better. That's something I learned, and he needs to see it, too.

"He needs to meet people who were treated like you. I'm thinking he needs to meet you."

I went numb.

"Say, Jimmy John, what's the matter? Change your mind?"

I couldn't speak at first. I couldn't move. Then I croaked, "You won't be sorry Cpl. Charley. You won't be sorry. Thank the good Lord we met. You won't be sorry."

20
Faith and Freedom

The next afternoon, after roll call, I heard a rumble on the road and hurried to the gate. "Foragers must be back early from gettin' food," I remember thinking.

Instead, a wagon arrived at the guard post. A man in regular clothes stepped down with a box and a three-legged stand. The guard called over another soldier and he and the visitor walked into the colonel's tent.

The visitor came out and waved to his driver, who tied the horses to a tree and got them water and feed. He helped to set up the stand near a tree with the tents in the background. He set the box on the stand.

I decided maybe it was some kind of game. These soldiers were good at that.

The men nearby acted excited and went to their tents. They came out wearing their full uniforms and caps on and took up their rifles. They stood by the tree alone, or in twos or threes, with their gun butts resting on the ground and their arms on each other's shoulders.

The first visitor leaned into the box and put a black cloth over his head. Believe me, I jumped pretty good when a flash like from a rifle came from the box. But the soldiers looked glad. Then he waved.

"Who's next?" he called. Another couple of soldiers came forward.

Cpl. Charley stood next to me.

"That's a camera he's looking into. Want your picture taken with me?"

Wasn't sure what he was talking about, but he was smiling, so I nodded.

We walked over to the bench by the tree and sat down. The man moved us around a little and walked back to his camera. "Don't move until I tell you," he called, and put that cloth over his head again.

"Look down or to the side a little," Charley said. "Don't let the flash surprise you."

I sat still, hardly breathing. I didn't dare even blink. The light flashed. After a minute, the man came out from under the black cloth, waved, and called, "Next!"

We got up and other men jumped in front of the camera. Some were standing and some sat on the bench.

"That photographer is one of a lot visiting the battlefields and camps to take pictures for the folks back home," Charley said. "We're lucky this one was shooting the infantry today. Mostly they pay attention to the officers."

We saw the photograph a little later. In it, Charley was looking off to the side, I was looking down, just like he said I should. Charley checked the picture, nodded, and handed it to me. "Your first photograph, Jimmy John. But there will be a lot more in your lifetime, I bet."

I put it carefully in the haversack Giles had given me. I wanted nuthin' to happen to it.

Life in camp for the next couple of weeks was about the way it was when I first saw it with the wagon driver and Giles. Then things changed, and quick. After roll call late one afternoon, the men of the Corps ate a big roasted beef meal, then pulled up stakes. The cooks packed wagonloads of food.

The soldiers packed hardtack and meat they could eat on the march.

Rumors pretty much settled on the idea that we was heading for Raleigh, way far from where I had ever been.

In the field where the sutlers set up business, Henry Davis and the others hurried to pack tents and wagons.

I helped Giles and the cooks. I looked over at my people grouped together farther back. I half wished I could be with them. But I figured it would be a good idea to stay near this Yankee corporal. I didn't want him to change his mind about me.

Especially not since the talk we had the day before with Henry Davis.

I was with the corporal and Will near the mule corral, cleaning rifles when Mr. Davis came over.

Half smiling, the sutler asked, "You sure you want to come up North to stay, Jimmy John?"

I thought about the plantation, which was not really home, and about my family, spread all over. I thought of my father, who might not be alive now.

"No reason to stay in North Carolina," I answered, rubbing oil into a gun stock. "I got my Cloak of Freedom when this Union army done come into Goldsboro and I aim to see where that takes me."

The sutler laughed, and the corporal frowned at him.

"Jimmy John, we have to think about some realities," Cpl. Charley said.

"I want to take you with me, but I'm not sure where you can stay. I'm not even a hundred percent sure where I'll stay.

"Remember I left home when I was still sixteen. About your age. I slept in the same bed with my brother. We had a big family, and I'm not a kid anymore. Where do I fit in?"

Will interrupted. "Maybe a bedroll on the floor? Like now?"

Charley snorted. "Bedrolls will be history when I get home. I'm gonna get me the best, softest, warmest goose down bed they make.

"Seriously, I don't even know if I have a job. What happens when all our boys go home? From Norwalk alone, there are 800, maybe 1,000, soldiers and sailors serving in this war. Will we all have jobs?"

Me, I knew nuthin' about city life. Especially city life in the North. I heard stories from Marse about the rich North and the factories that built the weapons and machines. I only knew about the plantation and the town where the Missus bought things we couldn't grow. I wanted to go North, yet what could I do in the city? I could barely write my name.

I bent over the gun and rubbed the stock with the rag like there was a genie inside to give me some answers.

I could feel the sutler's eyes on me. Then he spoke.

"I got a small piece of property in Wilton, about seven miles from South Norwalk. Not big enough to call a farm, maybe, but I plant corn for my animals. My brother is keeping things going while I'm in this war."

He laughed. "I don't know what shape it's in now. We never thought I'd be traveling with the army for four years, and by now he could be thinking he owns that land. Or maybe it's grown wild. He could have taken the animals over to his place and let the land go fallow.

"That's something I'll settle when we get home.

"Assuming I still have my own place, maybe you'd want to settle there, for room and board. Help me get it running the way it should be."

I jumped up.

"Mr. Davis, I could be the best farmhand you ever had. Thank you. Thank you, Jesus!"

I danced a little jig. Couldn't help it.

Giles grinned and shook his head. "Don't break a leg over it."

I ran off to tell other blacks, then sobered down. They was quiet after the news. I could see they had no idea of what would happen to them, or even if Gen. Sherman would let them go with the army much farther. And if they could go North, I wondered, would it be as bad as Marse said?

I made up my mind to stay close to the corporal and the sutler. Maybe that sutler, who liked to joke, was being serious now.

"You sound like a Christian believer, Jimmy John," Cpl. Charley said. "Did you go to church in Bear Creek?"

"We didn't have our own church. Missus had us come to the white church and sit in the back. When we could, we held our own service in the woods where we would pray for freedom.

"Are you a church goer, Cpl. Charley?" I asked him before, and he didn't answer back then.

The corporal shrugged. "The family goes to the Methodist Episcopal church. We have a Baptist church, too. There are others. I don't know much about them."

Henry shook his head. "I don't follow church religion, unless those Rebels are firing at us. Then praying comes naturally." He winked.

I watched Mr. Davis. He was friendly enough, and maybe he was close to the Lord, but his eyes sometimes seemed mocking. Soldiers said he sometimes cheated. Plenty owed him a good piece of their paychecks.

The corporal took me aside.

"Henry probably can give you a job, but you'll have to watch yourself."

"I know, Cpl. Charley. I know."

South Norwalk, 1917

I shook myself out of my memories and looked up at the big round clock on the wall.

"There I go again," I said to the boys. I was surprised they didn't let out a peep the whole time I was talking. "Get me started on that time, and I never stop talking."

"What happened then?" Willy asked. "Is that when you came here?"

I stood up and straightened slowly, wincing at my stiffness.

"Some important things happened first. We'll get to them next time. Ezra is ready to close up now." I nodded over to the janitor, leaning against the wall by the door.

"Good listenin,' " Ezra said on the way out. "Wagon's waitin' for us."

Alone later in my house down the road from the Hallock family home, I warmed up some chicken and rice and sat in my easy chair to think about those long ago days in Goldsboro.

When I talked about my Cloak of Freedom to Charley and Giles, I never dreamed it would take me to so many places: Virginia, Washington, New York, Connecticut, Massachusetts. Places I didn't even know the names of, back on the plantation.

I learned to really read and write, registered to vote, married, and became a father.

And then the great yearning grew inside to help build a church where my brothers and sisters could worship on the main floor and not only in the back or in the balcony.

Charley spoke up for me in Norwalk, sponsored me and sometimes counseled me. And let me be what I wanted to be. The sutler wasn't exactly honest about how he would treat me, but he gave me a chance to meet other people who liked my hard work.

The day of the next tutoring hour, I opened a box of keepsakes, took out a card, and wrapped it carefully. I put it in my jacket pocket before Ezra came by to drive me to the church. And I got to thinking about those last days I spent in the Confederate States of America.

21

An April to Remember

Rumors at the Goldsboro camp said the army would meet Gen. Grant at Richmond to end the war once and for all. But when Gen. Sherman returned from his meeting with the general, and some said with President Lincoln himself, the plan changed. And changed again.

This time Sherman's Army of Georgia would go after Gen. Joseph Johnston and his Army of Tennessee. We heard this Southern army was ragged and starving but still loyal to their general and the CSA. It was camped near Smithfield, about twenty-three miles north of us.

I watched the corporal's face as the detail checked the ammunition and cleaned their guns again. They settled into tending the animals and the supply wagons, amusing themselves, and waiting.

Cpl. Charley looked distracted.

"It's time to end this business," he said.

We heard all kinds of rumors about where the army really was heading. The latest talk was a march to Petersburg, a distance the men could cover in a day, if they had to. Then they could hook up with Gen. Grant.

Then a messenger rode into camp on Thursday, April 6, with news we all waited so long to hear—Gen. Grant had taken Richmond. The Rebel capital now flew the Union flag.

The camp exploded with cheers.

"Four long years of fighting and marching and marching and fighting," Cpl. Charley said. "It seems too good to be true. And yet it is."

"So the North has won?" I asked.

"Almost," he said. "We got the capital, but not the armies. Grant is still fighting Lee, and we're still after Johnston, this time to be sure he doesn't escape. If he does, we could be chasing his army all over the South for who knows how long."

Monday, Gen. Sherman's army was all smiles as they packed, set up the line of march of skirmishers, cavalry, artillery, infantry, supply wagons, horses and mules.

Thousands of my brothers and sisters still trailed behind.

The army stretched in a line seven miles down the road and then split apart into left, right and center divisions.

"That's so's we can confuse and catch the enemy," the corporal said. "Just as we did on the March to the Sea."

Cpl. Charley's Corps took the left fork, marching toward the railroad bridge by Smithfield. We reached the town the next day, but Gen. Johnston's army had escaped twenty miles north to Raleigh, burning the bridges along the way.

I joined my brothers helping the soldiers with the repairs. When we was done, the army was called to assembly once more.

Standing tall and smiling, Lt. Col. Henry Daboll read a statement from Gen. Sherman:

"The general commanding announces to the Army that he has official notice from Gen. Grant that Gen. Lee surrendered to him his entire army on the ninth, at Appomattox Court-House, Virginia.

"Glory to God and our country, and all honor to our comrades in arms, toward whom we are marching!

"A little more labor, a little more toil on our part, the great race is won, and our Government stands regenerated, after four long years of war."

If the colonel said anything else, I could hear none of it. The men was cheering and hurrahing, rolling on the ground laughing, thanking God, slapping each other's back, toasting with swigs from hidden canteens of whiskey.

"The war's over now?" I asked when I could get a word in.

"Almost, almost," Charley said. "There are other Confederate generals out there who might want to still fight. Others are leading troops in Alabama, Georgia, Florida, Louisiana and Texas.

"They may be hard to win over. We hear that the CSA President, Jefferson Davis, wants no more surrenders."

The soldiers had the wildest celebration I ever saw. They acted like they were crazy, all day and into the night.

More news came a few days later.

We heard on April 13 that leaders from the city of Raleigh rode a locomotive with a flag of truce to meet up with Gen. Sherman. They asked him to spare the city, and the general agreed. He set up his headquarters there.

"New orders," Cpl. Charley said to his foragers the next day as the left wing set up to move out.

"We go for food only, no destruction of railroads or factories without an army commander's permission. And we are to be more considerate of the poor, and not take everything they own.

"We're coming to the end of the countdown, boys. We know we're winning, and the commanders want us to pull back a little."

I didn't want to think anymore. What was really happening was bigger than anything I could have dreamed up. The Army reached Raleigh. The men knew by rumor and by what they saw and heard, that Union and Rebel generals already were talking to each other. The taste of victory was getting more real.

On April 17, Cpl. Charley told me that Gen. Sherman boarded a locomotive-driven rail car at eight o'clock in the morning for a two-hour ride to Durham Station. From there, he rode on horseback with Gen. Judson Kilpatrick of the cavalry and an escort with a white flag. A Confederate unit and Gen. Johnston, camped nearby at Hillsboro, met them.

The generals talked together in a farmhouse at Bentonville. Later, Gen. Sherman returned to his headquarters. Cpl. Charley said he heard only that terms of a surrender were talked about, and the two generals would meet again in the next few days.

The next time the colonel again called the soldiers to assembly, Will predicted the war was finally over. But after one look at the colonel, fighting back tears, we knew that something was wrong. He held up a paper.

"Men, I never thought I would have to read a message like this from the General." He cleared his throat and after a moment began to read:

"The general commanding announces, with pain and sorrow, that on the evening of the fourteenth instant, at the theater in Washington city, his Excellency the President of the United States, Mr. Lincoln, was assassinated."

Assassinated.

Before Gen. Sherman even met with Gen. Johnston.

Panicked, I looked around at the men around me. They stood still as statues.

Assassinated.

The colonel read more. The paper said that the murder involved conspirators who also attacked other leaders.

Secretary of State William Seward was stabbed in his head and his son was wounded.

The vice president was a target, but the man who was supposed to kill him backed out at the last minute.

Gen. Grant and his wife was supposed to go to the theater, but could not attend. They was safe.

An attack on the nation's leaders themselves.

The corporal bowed his head. The joy of the past days was gone, just like that.

The men grabbed off their hats and bowed their heads. Tears washed down their faces. They liked the President, and had voted to re-elect him five months before. The officers, who fought back their own grief before the announcement. now wept openly.

My head was buzzing. Mr. Lincoln dead!

Agonized voices all around me was saying that Mr. Lincoln was the best man to lead the United States. They worried what would happen to the nation now. Some talked of revenge.

The colonel spoke again.

"We may have the weapons and we may wage the battles, but our President had the vision to keep this nation whole. It's up to us, more than ever, to get this battle over with, to make the Union strong again."

The restless and grieving army waited in Raleigh for the next step. The men listened to my brothers and sisters singing our gospel songs and asked for more.

They read sad letters from home.

Cpl. Charley's mother sent him a letter with a copy of *The Gazette*. He read the letter and the newspaper, its front page framed in black, to the detail and to Giles and me.

Norwalk and South Norwalk joined to hold a procession on April 19 to honor the murdered President. "Just about everybody was on one committee or other to plan our observance," she wrote. "Everything went off smoothly and reverently on this beautiful, bright Wednesday that began with worship services and muffled bells at all the churches and lasted till near sunset."

He read how the march was marked with the firing of guns every half hour from morning until four o'clock that afternoon from Town House Hill in Norwalk and the rear of the Methodist Parsonage in South Norwalk.

All the stores was draped in black. The Bank of Norwalk stopped its clock at 7:22. A sign over it read, "The Nation's Saddest Hour." The march began at Union Park at Mott Avenue, circled through South Norwalk, over the Norwalk Bridge, up to the Norwalk Town Green and down again to the park.

The military light guards and militia company marched with arms reversed. Firemen draped their trucks in black bunting. The Phoenix Hose carriage was decorated on the side with a picture of President Lincoln. All the civic groups marched.

A funeral wagon, twelve feet long, seven feet wide and four feet high, topped by a bier draped in black and white and covered by a large flag, was drawn by twelve black horses, each led by a black man dressed in black.

Charley stopped reading. He bent his head and pressed his fingers to his wet eyes.

I stood next to him and said softly, "If that's your home town, Cpl. Charley, that's where I want to be."

A week later, the end of the war was official. Gen. Johnston agreed to the same terms as Gen. Lee and surrendered his army and all other confederate forces in North Carolina, South Carolina Georgia and Florida. Cpl. Charley said the total was 89,270 soldiers, the largest surrender of the war.

He said the generals defied their president, who wanted the war to continue to the death. Both generals said they wanted no more bloodshed. More men—623,026, and some said, even more—died in this war than in all the others combined.

After the surrender, Gen. Sherman ordered the army to stand with respect to the hungry and ragged Southern soldiers stiff at attention facing them. He issued the Confederates ten days' rations and sent them home with horses and mules so's they could grow their crops. There was to be no arrests.

"Finally I can answer your question with a yes, Jimmy John," the corporal said, with a quiet, far-off look so different from the carryings-on before the President was killed. "The war has ended."

The Union infantry and the artillery units soberly turned in their ammunition, except for ten rounds per man. The piles heaped high in Raleigh's public market.

22
Back Through Destruction

South Norwalk, 1918

I moved from the house to the porch rocker to wait for Ezra. The April air was warm this day, now fifty-three years after the end of that war. Leaves sprouted on every tree.

The boys and their questions about my own teen days helped to keep my thoughts of my friend alive since his death last September, just two days before he would have turned seventy-three.

The boys knew about the Civil War as a part of history. I knew it as the beginning of my real life. They knew about the great Abraham Lincoln, but they couldn't guess what slavery had been, or the joy of freedom, even with the hardships of days after we were finally no longer slaves.

I heard Ezra's horse and wagon come up the hill. I stepped to the curb.

We rode out from the crowded roads around Cliff Street down past the yellow brick First Methodist Episcopal Church, standing since the turn of the century, with its grand stained glass windows on wide, busy West Avenue.

Back when I first came to Norwalk, I went to services in the older church, sitting in the balcony with the other black members. I walked the seven miles every week from my bosses' homes in Wilton, and Rowayton, until I took jobs in factories or worked at odd jobs in Norwalk. I lived in rented rooms in South Norwalk until I could buy a home of my own. Small, maybe, but mine.

My community now prayed in a rented building on Knight Street, about a mile north of the big yellow church.

"We're almost there," Ezra said, as turned left on Knight Street.

"Soon we can say we're heading to a church building we actually own," I said with pride. Through the decades, I worked as treasurer to meet that dream. The building fund was growing slowly, steadily. My prayer was to make it a reality in my lifetime. Lord knows, we was getting closer.

At the church, I spent some time answering letters and preparing for the weekend service with the minister. My door was open to visitors, and sure enough, Jesse soon stood there.

"Deacon?" he called softly.

I looked up. "How are you, Jesse? Be right with you. I was looking forward to seeing you today."

I pushed the papers aside and we walked down the hall to the meeting room where a half dozen boys sat at the table, chattering.

I slipped into my chair in the middle of them. They went quiet, expectant.

"I want to show you something."

I pulled the packet from my pocket and took out a photograph mounted on heavy cardboard.

"Remember I told you that the corporal and I had our picture taken together in Goldsboro? Well, here we are."

The boys crowded around. The black and white photograph was an oval in a rectangle. They saw a lean white man with a dark floppy hat raked over one eye. His shirt was open at the neck, and he wore a wrinkled jacket. It didn't look much like a uniform. He had a mustache and looked off to the side with a serious glance. He was almost twenty-one, but he looked maybe ten years older.

Next to him was a serious black boy with wide-set eyes in a round face and a light cap tilted to the right. Me. I had on a loose, collarless shirt and baggy pants.

"That's you, Deacon?" Jesse asked. "You was fifteen there?"

"I know what you're thinking," I chuckled. "That child is too young to be fifteen. But Jesse, stand up.

The boy rose.

"See, you're twelve and almost taller than me now. It's just the way it is."

I took the picture and carefully folded it back inside the paper.

"I once thought I'd frame this, but then thought it would fade in the daylight. So I just take it out from my dresser at home to look at it now and then.

"I'm proud to say my friend here wanted a picture for himself. A couple of days after we got to South Norwalk we went to a photographer in town to make a copy of this one.

"The corporal kept it all his life in his parlor, with his other war reminders, like his Twentieth Corps patch and a Confederate dollar bill and a square of hardtack preserved under glass.

"But anyway, in our talk today, we're up to the part where both the corporal and I was about to

220

take the greatest journey of our lives. That's the march from Raleigh."

We left Raleigh on April 30, 1865. It was a warm and sunny Sunday. Cpl. Charley joked that Nature was finally on our side, and that the trees and flowers was looking their best.

"Even the rivers we pass over seem pleased that this awful war is over."

The army marched nearly one hundred sixty miles to Richmond, and a little more than a hundred to Alexandria, outside Washington. The march in the heat was hard, but the men didn't seem to notice much.

Gen. Williams had us on the road each day before dawn. We halted during the hottest hours and started up again when the air cooled up some. The army moved north about twenty miles a day.

I tried to keep up with the powerful and fit marchers, but soon Cpl. Charley ordered a mule for me to ride.

"Thank you. My feet thank you."

We passed open fields that Cpl. Charley said was once divided by fences before the armies came through. The trees was all shattered from artillery shells and musket balls. The ground was messed up by years of marching feet, cannon caissons, wagons, horses and mules. The men murmured quietly as they passed through familiar places.

In some towns, we met only women and children and old men. Men young enough to fight had gone to war and few came back. Farms was abandoned, except that some former slaves was tending small plots.

Our marchers met up with Rebel soldiers heading south. This time, there was no fighting. They mingled and talked about where they fought and where they was going. I saw some Union soldiers pass on part of their rations to the Southerners.

"Uncle Billy told those men in Atlanta that things would be different after the war was over," Cpl. Charley said later. "I didn't understand then, but now I don't feel anger toward these soldiers. They also fought for what they thought was right.

"Except we were more right," he said. "We were protecting the time all those years ago when we fought together to boot out the British and create this country together. It has to stay united to be strong. And we were fighting for you, although we didn't always know it."

He shook his head. "But you know, Jimmy John, I sometimes think the men of both armies could have settled issues if they were asked, without the awful toll of war."

Maybe, but he never met Marse.

The regiment stopped near Manchester to collect rations and then the engineers set out a pontoon bridge over the James River. "Boys, look, Belle Isle, over to the left," Cpl. Charley called out. The men stared grimly at the Confederate prison, where Cpl. Charley said 30,000 Union soldiers had been prisoners of war and more than 1,000 starved or died of disease. He said this year, Union forces took over and turned it into a prison for Confederate officers and soldiers awaiting parole, with black Union soldiers in charge.

I could only wonder about that, especially when Cpl. Charley said that in battle, black Union soldiers was treated badly by the Rebels, who looked on them as slaves still.

We camped one midday near Spotsylvania, and Charley, Will and I fell in with a group that decided to tour the battlefield.

"Cpl. Charley, look! Skeletons!" I shrank back.

"I heard Grant pulled out in such a hurry that he didn't even have time to bury the dead. So it was true."

We passed the Wilderness, where Cpl. Charley said Gen. Grant fought just before Spotsylvania in 1864, and walked through Chancellorsville. The two battlefields was a mess of burned underbrush more than three miles long, where some soldiers was fiercely killed.

Cpl. Charley spoke very quietly. "I still can't think of Chancellorsville without having nightmares. The officers lost that battle. The boys were never defeated."

I remembered how Marse gloated over those victories.

The men assembled again back at camp and together we crossed over the Rappahannock River. The next day we camped near Cattett's Station on the Orange & Alexandria Railroad.

The army went on to revisit Battle Run Creek, their Fairfax Station campground, the Fairfax and Alexandria Pike to Fairfax Seminary. Lots of places I couldn't imagine.

"We were so green then," Cpl. Charley said. "And our volunteer officers were just as inexperienced." Then he grinned and punched Will on the arm. "Good thing we seasoned some before we caught up with the likes of you."

Will rubbed his arm. "Ungrateful! You needed us, to tell us how useless we were."

We went into camp three miles from Alexandria, near Fort Worth. Cpl. Charley calculated that since Savannah in January, the Corps marched for seven hundred sixty-two miles. I believed him. Just in the last twenty days, we marched two hundred and sixty miles from Raleigh to Alexandria.

The camp days was lazy and boring and the men talked all the time about home. They answered roll call three or four times a day. Sometimes Cpl. Charley and Will got passes to visit Alexandria.

The men mostly drilled to get into shape for the Grand Review in Washington.

Yet Gen. Sherman didn't want the men to be too "spit and polish." Only necessary clothing was issued. He said he wanted the people to meet this army as it was in the long hard battles since Atlanta—rough and confident.

Cpl. Charley smiled when he heard the order. "Uncle Billy had everything right," he said.

23
Grand Review

Wednesday, May 24, the soldiers was up before dawn, whistling and polishing their weapons again. They was in real good spirits. Only natural, because this was the big day when the brass in Washington D. C. would meet the Army that marched across Georgia.

We broke camp. The Twentieth Corps was to be third in the line of march, behind the Army of the Tennessee and the Fifteenth Corps. Gen. Sherman ordered the men to carry a supply of cooked rations in their haversacks, so they knew to expect a long day.

I was busting my skin. I was free, and could celebrate with the men who brought me from the fields and swamps where I had lived all my life as somebody's property.

Now here I was, almost in Washington D.C., the Number One city in the country, where I would see President Andrew Johnson with my own eyes. He wasn't President Lincoln, but he was the President.

We heard that the crowds gave a mighty good welcome to Gen. George Meade's Army of the Potomac the day before. His 80,000 men took eight hours to pass the reviewing stand. They was watched by Gens. Johnson and Grant, commanding general of all the Union Armies, and a bunch of national, state, military, and foreign officials.

Folks called out the names of units and officers as they passed. Everybody knew them for what they did in and around Virginia.

"Humph," Cpl. Will complained. "Sure, they got all the notice in the local papers because they marched and fought around Richmond and Washington, while we slogged through nasty swamps no one ever heard of, hundreds of miles away."

"We'll hold our own today," Cpl. Charley said. "We've drilled enough in these last days to put on a respectable show. Besides, Uncle Billy has found a way to show the people that we're survivors of a different kind of war. The battles in Tennessee and our March to the Sea and the Carolinas Campaign were a whole other experience, and they'll see the men who pulled that off."

Cpl. Charley turned to me.

"Jimmy John, we'll need you and Giles and some of the others to help manage the mules and other animals in the rear once the parade starts. No telling how they'll act once they move along city streets. Then we'll be together after the review."

He patted my shoulder. I saluted, and looked for Giles.

It was a fine Spring day for us, just as it had been for Gen. Meade's army.

The Army of the Tennessee was waiting just north of Pennsylvania Avenue. The men stepped off and the Fifteenth Corps of the Army of Georgia waited for their signal at Alexandria, across the Long Bridge over the Potomac. The Twentieth Corps moved up in line to be next across the bridge.

Long before we could see anything across the river, we could hear the music from the brigade and field bands ahead of us. We could hear the roar of the crowds.

The men fiddled with their slouch hats bearing the red star of the First Division, Twentieth Corps. They smoothed their coats, so weather-beaten that they seemed almost gray instead of blue. They rubbed their mustaches or their bearded faces and longish hair. They fidgeted and joked during the long wait.

The sun was already high in the sky when we began to move. We crossed the bridge, and now the sound was deafening.

I looked up into the crowds with so many feelings in my brain and heart. It was a wonder. People, clapping and calling out, packed the sidewalks as far as I could see on both sides of the wide avenue. Buildings was covered in red, white, and blue. People leaned out of windows and balconies, waving flags and flowers.

The men spread out to twelve across when they reached the domed Capitol and stepped off down Pennsylvania Avenue.

The flag bearer unfurled the tattered Corps flag and the men shouldered their arms. Bayonets flashed in the sunlight.

Our Fifth Connecticut Regiment led off the division, followed by the Third Wisconsin and the Second Massachusetts, the regiments that fought beside it in Georgia and the Carolinas.

They was followed by the Second Division and its flag with a white star, and the third, with the blue star. Their band struck up just as the last band of the Fifteenth Corps went silent up the avenue. The men kept their eyes straight ahead but marched with a swagger, and the crowd roared in excitement.

I could see the huge reviewing stand far ahead, in front of the President's House, which some people called the White House. At a signal, the infantry turned their faces to the stand. President Johnson, Gens. Grant, Meade, and Sherman, with a wreath of red flowers around his neck, and members of the government, beamed back at them.

The crowds kept calling out the names of the President and the generals, who kept standing to take bows. For six hours, bands played and colors dipped.

The crowd was silent after the three divisions of the Twentieth passed. The people stared in curiosity when they saw us freed slaves, followed by foragers and the animals. Then they roared in excitement.

It was a mighty experience. All those people cheering, even for us. Like they was happy for us. My Cloak of Freedom was light on my shoulders.

After the parade, the armies marched out of the capitol. The Twentieth went another eight miles to Bladensburg and set up camp for the night. Then we moved on to Fort Stevens, the site where President Lincoln nearly was attacked by Confederate Maj. Gen. Jubal Early the year before. From Fort Stevens we went into camp at the Piney Branch Trotting Course.

That's when Mr. Davis and I heard some good news and I ran to tell Cpl. Charley.

"You hear about the people who killed the President? They was hanged!" I felt like my eyes was poppin' out of my head. We went back to the sutler's wagon and Mr. Davis handed over the local paper, filled with news of the trial and the hangings.

"The timing couldn't have been better," Cpl. Charley said when he put down the paper. "Now it really is over."

Still, we spent another two months around Alexandria. The regiment was assigned to the Twenty-second Army Corps in the Brigade Bartlett Division Defenses of Washington, with the One Hundred Forty-Third New Jersey, Forty-Sixth Pennsylvania and Second Massachusetts Regiments. Mostly now, the men marched every day in Dress Parade reviews and one night in a candlelight parade.

They was mustered out July 19, three days short of their swearing in four years earlier. They broke camp July 21, said quick goodbyes to the men they fought beside all those years, and headed for the train station in Washington.

We waited some more once we got there. We rested in the dirt under the hot sun until some freight cars was backed into the station to take on the Fifth and four small New York regiments.

I sat with Cpl. Charley and Cpl. Will on top of the car. It was hot, but not as hot as inside.

I squirmed around to get comfortable.

"Congratulations, Jimmy John, you have the honor to head North in true soldier style," Cpl. Will said.

At Baltimore we moved over to the train for New York City. This time we had better cars and rode inside.

"I'm going home," Cpl. Charley murmured, looking out his window. "How many days, months, years, did I think that might never happen."

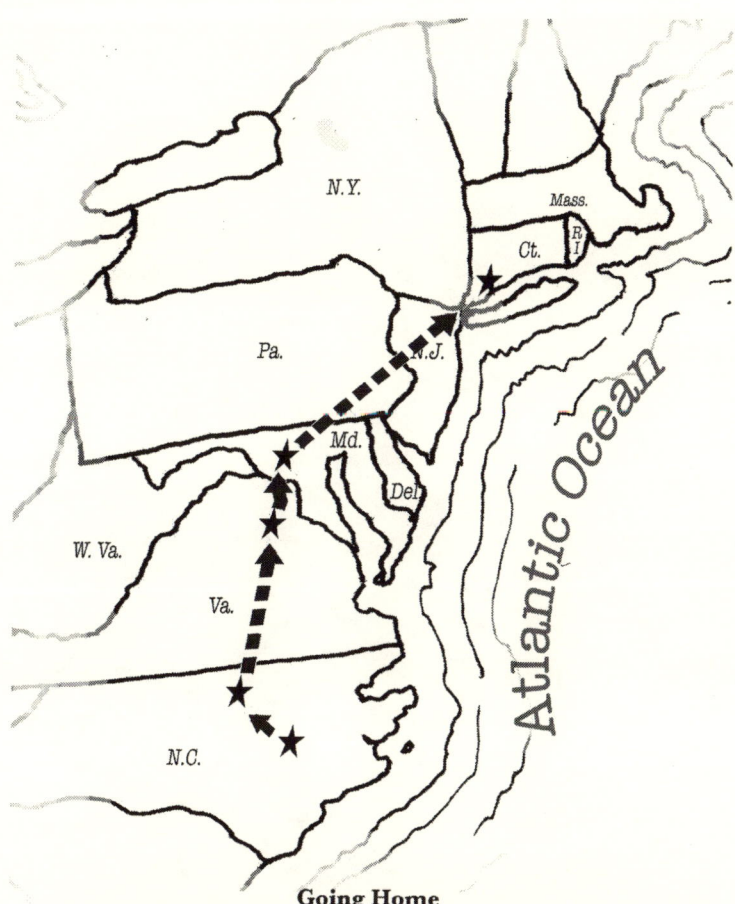

Going Home

The army left Goldsboro, N.C. April 30, 1865 and marched 320 miles to Washington, D.C., averaging 20 miles a day. After the Grand Review, Charley and Jimmy John rode another 273 miles by train to South Norwalk, Ct.

24
New Beginnings

I stuck to Cpl. Charley and Cpl. Will like glue. and I sat on the floor with them, at the end of a car. They was down to the final friends heading to different parts of New England.

"You realize we're likely to never see these boys again?" Cpl. Will said. "Of course, that's pretty good in some cases, but I'd kinda like to know how the others get along." He went silent.

"I've been thinking about all that since before Alexandria," Cpl. Charley said. "Right up there with the wounded that made it back home, and so many who didn't."

"Cpl. Charley, what will you do now?" I asked.

"That's another thing. I'm not Corporal anything any more. Just Mr. Charles F. Hallock, a filer for The Norwalk Lock Company. Hopefully."

"And I'm not Jimmy John any more."

Will cocked his head and looked at me, questioning.. "And who are you, then?"

"I'm Mr. John D. Taylor, freedman, out of North Carolina."

"Mr. Taylor?"

"That's right. That's now my family name. You could say it's an old family name."

"Hm," murmured Charley. "And Mr. Taylor, are you still interested in working as a farmhand for room and board at Henry Davis's place?"

"Yessir. That hasn't changed. Just my Cloak of Freedom has made me a new man.

"Cpl., er, Mr. Charley, you ever think of sometime visiting some of the men from Pennsylvania or Ohio or Wisconsin you fought with?

He shrugged. "Can't say. Can't say I won't even visit back down South sometime, to see where these four years went. Might even like to see Gettysburg again. In the far distant future, though. Right now I want to go home, set my bags down in my folks' house on Flax Hill and not move any time soon. I've traveled enough for a lifetime."

"Not me," I said. "I never went anywhere because I couldn't, and now I want to see as much as I can. Why, I just put on my new name and I've been in a half-dozen states already."

He interrupted me. "Just remember. Old ideas take a long time to die. You could see that, in the way black soldiers were paid less in our Army, and even after the war they were not allowed to march in the Grand Review."

"You know, Charley, we're not quite free yet, either," Will interrupted. "We can't put that uniform in mothballs right away. We're set to march—again—in a parade to celebrate our homecoming.

"Charley slumped down further and pushed his cap over his eyes. "In that case, I'm getting some shut-eye."

South Norwalk, 1918

Sitting in my house in South Norwalk, my eyes filled with remembering. I thought a lot now about those early days of the beginning of the rest of my life.

Charley took me home for his family to meet me. He put our photograph on the side table in the sittingroom, right next to a picture of Will and some of the others. And next to that he had that square of hardtack, and the Confederate dollar bill.

Neighbors stepped in when they saw Henry Davis wasn't treating me right, and one of them hired me away to tend his own property, this time not for just room and board. Real money wages. In time I was hired by others. I even worked in factories in South Norwalk. I married and started a family. I bought the house I live in now.

All the while, I attended church and thanked the Lord every time I could for what He had done for me. First it was Charley's church. Then I and other brothers and sisters decided to have a church of our own, a place where we didn't have to sit in the balcony. We joined the African Methodist Episcopalians and held services in the Norwalk Town Hall and now on Knight Street.

I became treasurer of the fund to get our building. We was seeing progress. The Good Lord heard my prayers and I worked hard to become a deacon.

Charley stayed a good friend, guiding me, encouraging me. We spoke sometimes about the war. He said his hard experiences had taught him a lot about the people the army was fighting for and against. Mostly, he said, people on both sides were a lot alike.

Now, more than fifty years later, our country entered the World War in Europe. American boys left their homes for France. They had a cause and maybe they were a little excited at first to see places they only read about.

Some of those boys were Norwalkers, neighbors. I felt some of the closeness and pain of losing friends, like Charley talked about. Wish I could talk with him about that.

One fine fall day, I asked Ezra to drive me to the cemetery before he took me home.

"I want to pay a visit, with the trees in all their gold and red glory," I told Ezra. "I want to see where Charley Hallock is resting."

We traveled the mile to Riverside Cemetery's stone entrance. I pointed out my own family tombstone, right by the office. My wife, Julia, gone some 25 years, was buried there.

We stopped a cemetery worker for directions and walked slowly up a path to the Hallock family plot. When I turned and looked down the hill, sure enough, my own stone marker was dead ahead, in plain sight.

I clapped my hands. Ezra's lips curved into a smile.

"Well, well," I said with satisfaction, "when it's my turn to rest beside my dear Julia, I expect Charley and I will be able to continue our conversation even better than when we was walking along the winding roads in his home town, in my town of freedom."

Acknowledgments

There were many helping hands in creating this historical novel, a work of fiction closely based on people and events in Norwalk, Connecticut, and the American Civil War, 1861-1865.

The story line follows events in the lives of Deacon John Taylor and Cpl. Charles F. Hallock, of the Connecticut Volunteers and of battles in the South, but fictional elements were used for dialogue, events and for some characters. Not much could be confirmed about Deacon Taylor's early life in North Carolina, where an archivist suggested Taylor may have changed his name to protect his family. I worked with examples of many slaves in choosing last names, as described by Paul Keroack, a Norwalk genealogist and Collection Manager for the Norwalk Library's History Room. The deacon's work and life after he arrived in South Norwalk were confirmed by church and state reference sources.

As to other assistance: Robert Tolles of New Canaan, and especially Blaikie Hines, author of "Civil War: Volunteer Sons of Connecticut" (American Patriot Press, Maine, 1949) provided key information about the Fifth Connecticut Volunteer Infantry. Thanks also to the New England Civil War Museum in Rockville, Conn., and Renae MacLachlan, Licensed Battlefield Guide, at the Gettysburg National Military Park. and to Isabel Bullen, former Norwalk librarian and author of "Norwalk's Carnegie Libraries" (Otter Bay Books, Maryland,

2013). Lugenia Shipp of the Bethel A.M.E. Church of Norwalk provided information about Deacon Taylor's work to create Norwalk's first black congregation. I'm grateful to Otha Brown Jr. (1931-2009) for his encouragement to write this story, and to John Hiscock, director, and his staff at the Second Taxing District Water Department of Norwalk, in making available records of the City of South Norwalk's Council before the city's consolidation with the City of Norwalk in 1913.

I also researched the archives and historical section of the Connecticut State Library, The Norwalk Historical Society, the New Canaan Library, the New Canaan Historical Society, the Wilton Library and the Wilton Historical Society, the town clerk records of Norwalk and Wilton.

Most of all, I relied on the memoir and other writings of C. F. Hallock, and on his obituary in The Hour; on military accounts of battles online and the online autobiography of Gen. William Tecumseh Sherman; and on "Norwalk: Being an historical account of that Connecticut town," by Deborah Wing Ray and Gloria P. Stewart (Phoenix Publishing, New Hampshire, 1979).

All in all, this work of fiction was as true as I could make it.

My thanks also go to Eileen Harrington, Matthew Hallock, John and Louise Frank, Ruth Jannson, and Bette Conner and the members of the Guilt Free Book Club for their input and suggestions.

Finally, this book was made possible through the support of my husband, Tony, and our sons, Tony III and Lt. Col Philip Mobilia, USMC.

About the Author

Dorothy Mobilia is a former newspaper reporter and editor for various publications in New York and Connecticut. She lives in Connecticut with her husband. This is her first novel.

Made in the USA
Charleston, SC
09 December 2014